Easterchicks Gone Bad

By Sheri Dixon

ISBN-13: 978-0615677569 (Sheri\Dixon)

Easterchicks Gone Bad is a collection of articles written by Sheri Dixon and reprinted with permission from www.homestead.org.

I dedicate this book to Neil, owner of Homestead.org.
Who nit-picked me into becoming a better writer.

To my friend Gale, whose impulse purchase of
dyed baby poultry made the very first story possible.

And to all those friends from around the world
who encouraged me to bind these all together in a
tangible, portable, tote-into-the-bathroom form

Here ya go. And thank you.

Table of Contents

Easterchicks Gone Bad- The Unexpected Menace

They looked innocent enough, like fuzzy giant skittles bouncing around the tub.

My friend had purchased colored Easterchicks for her daughters and had assumed that I would be thrilled to take them after Easter.

Why not?

We DO live in the country.

Thirteen brightly colored chicklets arrived at our place in a large cage. They were cute, they were fluffy, they were hungry.

They made endearing little noises when we fed them. We loved our chickens.

Before long, they had molted out of their Easter feathers and looked like real chickens. They were turned loose to free range and be the cherry on our country yard sundae.

The coyote in the woods also loved our chicks. In no time we were down to 8. Our only Rhode Island Red in the bunch wandered into the dog pen and we were down to 7.

One started to terrorize the cats and went to live with a friend. One chased our little boy and went to live with a neighbor.

Five chickens- 4 White Leghorn roosters and (we thought) a big Barred Rock hen.

The Barred Rock foraged into the goat pen and the Great Pyrenees decided she needed a bath. By the time I got out there she was gasping and dripping with dog drool. I turned her back into the yard, and she didn't join up with the other chickens right away, she just stalked up and down, mumbling chicken curses.

From that point on, she couldn't/wouldn't roost up in the tree with the others, but chose a low spot right next to the goat pen (go figure) to sleep in. We rested a piece of sheet metal against the fence to make a chicken tent.

About that time they entered poultry puberty. The roosters crowed roughly every 5 minutes all day long and most of the night. They started making little fighting runs at each other and I worried that they would kill each other.

That would be bad, because we loved our chickens.

I needn't have worried.

Before too long they stopped quarreling amongst themselves and turned all their energy on a common enemy- me, and by association, my son.

They were a Chicken Gang.

All they needed were little leather jackets, sunglasses, and packs of Camels (filterless of course) rolled up into their wings. They'd stand at the edge of the woods, daring the coyotes to come out. They cruised the neighborhood, lookin' for trouble, mean and restless.

I now know what the Raptors in the Jurassic Park movies are based on- roosters.

They have the same moves, calls and hunting tactics. They would sneak up behind me to attack, barking strategy to each other. If I turned around, they'd freeze and look off into the distance, casually.

I started carrying a broom.

They recognized my car and would come running at the sound of it. I tucked the broom under the car seat.

They would come onto the porch and stare at me through the glass door, growling.

I was beginning to dislike our chickens.

At first, my son just carried a big stick when he played outside. Since the roosters outnumbered him, after a while he only went out to play after they roosted in the evening.

He was becoming pale and alittle twitchy.

Invitations to our house became BYOB- Bring Your Own Broom.

It was time for the roosters to go.

We tried to catch them, but they were fast as greased lightning, very wary, and practiced survivors, being the ones who outlived coyotefest.

I ran an ad in the Thrifty Nickel that read-

Free Roosters.
White Leghorns, 7 months old.
Free Range. Mean as Snakes. You Catch.

The first 6 calls I got were not for the chickens, but for the stove we were giving away. (Read the ad again).

The 2 good ol' boys who attempted catching the roosters went away empty-handed, the taunting of the roosters ringing in their ears. Nabbing them while they were sleeping was difficult since they roosted way out on the limb of an oak tree 20 feet in the air.

I hated our chickens.

I began trying to run them down with the car as I drove into the yard. I could SEE them going under the car, but they always exploded out from behind, missing tail feathers, and screaming poultry death threats. One of them actually leaped up onto the hood of the car, glared at me through the windshield and crowed defiantly.

I loathed our chickens.

At long last, the son of a friend came after dark; perched atop the tallest stepladder we had, and plucked them neatly from the oak tree. The roosters were back in the cage they had first come in.

With the Fearsome Foursome behind bars, our "hen" started crowing. Lacy was really Larry. He has been warned that he's ridiculously easy to catch, living in a tent and all, so he'd better behave or he will suffer the same fate.

Like the idiot I am, now I pitied the chickens.

What to do with them?

The obvious answer- Kill them and eat them, is still beyond my ability. I KNOW they are just chickens, and we eat chicken all the time. I KNOW given weapons, opposable thumbs, and a nice gas grill, they would have no problem killing and eating us.

I just couldn't do it. Still working on that part of farming...

We couldn't give them away to lay siege to someone else’s yard.

We toyed with the idea of driving far away, finding a nice wild wooded spot, and setting them free. My husband even took to singing, "Bock Bock Bock Born Free...", but we were advised that they would have a bad environmental impact on the wilderness.

Finally, they went into the stewpot at a friend's father-in-law's house, an ignoble ending to what could have been a glorious life.

Poor chickens.

I didn't mind the constant crowing, the massive amounts of poop EVERYWHERE, the feathers. If they just hadn't been aggressive, they could've lived long and free for all of their chicken days.

Stupid chickens.

I feel sad, because, after all-

We loved our chickens.

BLACKTHUMB- Helpful Hints for the Cultivationally Challenged

Stoke up the fire; grab a mug of cocoa, your seed catalogs and your loved ones, for as sure as Christmas brings visions of Sugarplums, late winter brings visions of the Perfect Garden.

Over the course of the last 25 years, I have gardened both sides of the Mason-Dixon line, and I have compiled a Gardeners' list of Untruths, for those of us who have followed to the letter the advice of the" Master Gardeners", come up with nothing to serve our families but dust and weevils, and had our neighbors turn us in for suspected toxic waste storage (HEY, that's my garden!) Keep in mind that I have personally tested every Untruth, and while I will never claim to be a Good Gardener, I am comfortable in my role as Blackthumb, Defender of Inept Gardeners, Protector of Those Who Keep Trying.

Untruth #1- Rent the Rototiller and simply push it along, smiling and humming a settlers' tune as it turns your land into premium, glorious, farmland.

Truth- Pay someone with a real tractor to till up your garden plot. If you want to experience the effects of Rototilling on your body, have someone work you over with a sack of wet sand, then jump off of your garage roof. Naked. Into brambles.

Untruth #2- your veggies will look just like the picture in the catalog.
Truth- Actually, they WILL look just like the pictures; they just don't tell you that the pictures are life-size.

Untruth #3- Newspaper makes excellent mulch.
Truth- Newspaper looks like litter in your garden. Because it IS litter in your garden. The best mulch I ever used was stall innards from the goat pen, wheelbarrowed directly from pen to garden and dumped between rows. If you have no goats (I can help you with that), the thick black plastic the garden store sells is a good alternative that keeps out weeds and doesn't look awful. Last year's hay works well too, the flakes are about the right size to fit between rows.

Untruth #4- Fish heads make excellent fertilizer.
Truth- although legend has it that the Indians planted a fish head with every kernel of corn, the reality is that this is a myth perpetuated by generations of skunks looking for an easy meal.

Untruth #5- Natural pest control works just as well as chemical pest control.
Truth- There's nothing like a good dose of poison to kill bugs. Since my children had a habit of eating straight from the garden, I always go chemical-free, and assume the "one for me, two for nature" attitude. Although using beer for slugs does work. Taken internally by the gardener in a large enough dose to obliterate any thought of slugs.

Untruth #6- Mothballs/aluminum pie tins/sweaty shirts/Tabasco sauce/gunshots will deter mammalian pests.
Truth- the instant your sweet corn is ready to pick, some sort of silent Corn Alarm sounds, and nothing will keep the raccoons away. I witnessed the mid-day destruction of my sweet corn from 20 feet away, yelling, waving my arms, jumping up and down and lobbing every liftable object at the masked darlings. They totally ignored the Crazy Woman at the edge of the garden (you would think rabies would've been a concern, I was certainly foaming at the mouth), bent a stalk, opened an ear, took 3 or 4 bites, then

moved onto the next one, effectively ruining the entire crop and breaking my heart simultaneously. There is nothing on earth as delicious as homegrown sweet corn, harvested and cooked within minutes, slathered with real butter. If I ever have the courage to plant sweet corn again, I will fence that area and turn a big doggie loose in it two weeks before harvest.

Untruth #7- Throwing netting over your fruit trees will keep the birds from eating your ripening fruit.
Truth- The birds actually love this one, as they hop up into your branches and can eat all day long without worrying about getting eaten themselves by a hawk.

Untruth #8- the catalogs are full of thousands of different veggies, so you must plant all of them.
Truth-Plant only what you will eat. Also, learn what you can plant together. I learned that if you plant cucumbers and gourds next to each other, you get mutants that are neither edible nor decorative, just disturbing.

Untruth #9- If your children help in the garden, they will be proud to eat the Fruits of Their Labor.
Truth- Kids are kids and kids hate veggies. This can also work against you when they name each tomato and you are not allowed to eat them either.

Untruth #9 1/2- Working together in the garden will enhance the sibling bond.
Truth- One year my daughter gave her little brother a radish, claiming it was a strawberry just to see the look on his face at the first bite. He fell for it every time. Yes. Every time. She is now in law school, and for years he harbored a grave suspicion of all food products.

Untruth #10- you will save a bundle on your grocery bill by growing your own produce.
Truth- After the tilling, purchasing and planting, mulching, fertilizing, pest deterring, watering, harvesting and putting up, you will be munching $10 carrots. My daughter did make a tidy sum

one year growing and selling pumpkins. We planted them amongst the rows of corn and they did well. This was in Wisconsin where the Yankee raccoons are more civil than these Southern Rebel raccoons and I could actually eat my own sweet corn and have enough left to freeze. (sigh)

To New Gardeners planning a first garden, these veggies are easy to grow and most likely to be eaten- green beans (get the bush type unless you want to build poles), tomatoes (get cages), squashes, cucumbers, corn (needs lots of room and a razor wire fence for protection).

Beware of zucchini. If you must grow it, buy a packet of seeds, plant one, and throw the rest away. You will still be slipping surplus zucchinis into strangers' purses just to get rid of the damn things.

This year we will again plant a garden, for Hope springs eternal, there is no finer workout than an hour or two in the garden, and country life just doesn't seem complete without those precious gems from your own garden- the one tomato that doesn't have rust, the one strawberry that doesn't have a resident slug, squash yellow as sunshine, corn sweet as candy.

Hand me that seed catalog, would you? I hear the call of the land. (Sounds suspiciously like giggling raccoons...)

Cutting the Utilical Cord- Part One- Turning the Tables on Reddy Kilowatt.

We've scrimped. We've saved. We've searched far and wide. At long last we're here- The Country.

Whether our Country is 100 acres in the center of the middle of nowhere, or nestled among other small homesteads of a few acres each, we take very seriously the stewardship of this precious land we have chosen to call Home Sweet Home.

Organic gardening? Of course.

Learning and/or perfecting farming crafts and skills? Absolutely.

Self-sufficiency is the core of the Apple of Homesteadery. Duh.

A few of us are settling virgin acres miles from conventional power, while most of us are building reasonably close to utility hookups or renovating old farmhouses with varying degrees of modernization.

The former group of Homesteaders has no choice- alternative energy is thrust upon them, and they have my undying admiration. Their task is huge, their dedication to the "simple" life inspiring, mainly because there is nothing simple about it.

I belong to the latter group; those of us who unthinkingly turn on the tap and water comes out, flip a switch and lights come on, adjust the thermostat and feel comfortable. We must consciously choose between conventional consumption and alternative, possibly less convenient but undeniably more Earth friendly utility options.

My family is at the point of choosing, and although we have never been accused of being "normal" or "average", I believe our findings and plans match many other contemporary Homesteaders'.

If you are looking for a really good, technical article on the science of photovoltaics, there are hundreds of them on the web and whole shelves of books devoted to that, but this ain't it. I don't necessarily need to know How this stuff works; I need to know Why it will work for my family and our tiny fragment of Earth. This is one old country gal who barely made it through high school science trying to gather enough basic knowledge to make sense and make a difference.

In a nutshell, here’s how it works-

Energy from the Sun is collected by solar panels. It's transported to batteries that store it, and from there it goes to an inverter that turns it into usable, garden-variety electricity. It then travels a) back into your house to power your stuff, or, in an inter-tie situation, b) back through the meter (which will run it BACKWARDS) and into the grid to run other peoples' stuff.

Disclaimer The following thoughts, ideas and plans are the express opinions of the Dixon family. Each family has their own level of comfort regarding utilities, and except for possibly using genetically enhanced hamsters on amphetamines running little power wheels, everyone's' opinions are correct for them, and to be respected. *End Disclaimer*

Our current utility situation includes city water, city sewer, conventional electric and natural gas hookups.

Our first task was to decide how much energy we wanted to cover, and our confident albeit naive answer was "Hey, since we are going to do it, why not do it up right? Let's produce ALL our electricity with the help of Old Sol."

Next, we needed to look at our existing electrical usage (egads!). Using a handy worksheet I downloaded from RealGoods, we ascertained that during our high-usage months, we use just shy of 80,000-watt hours per day, or 2,400 kilowatts per month. This was verified by looking at our electric bill. Oh sure, I could've just looked at the bill and saved myself several hours lookin' under and behind stuff with my reading glasses, a flashlight, and a large shoe to squash creepy things, but the worksheet itemizes and highlights the power hogs. (Plus I now know where all the dust bunnies go when they die).

For a system to power our current house at our current usage using our high month figures, we would need to write a check for right around $100,000. Hmmmm, we need a Plan. This is obviously not one of those projects that can be tackled of a piece (unless I'm holding the winning Texas Lottery ticket).

Also, if we lived in the Austin TX area, AustinEnergy would pay us $5 per watt towards our installation. Given that cost is between $6 and $9 per watt, that's pretty sweet. My husband thinks it's reason enough to pack up and move to Austin, but he's always looking for an excuse to do that...

STEP ONE: we need to TURN STUFF OFF. I was assured that our electric usage was pretty standard for a house of our size, but that only made me feel worse, because I thought we already DID use less electricity than most folks. Just paying attention and turning stuff off will cut our usage by about 15%, according to Stephen the Technician at RealGoods.

STEP TWO: upgrade/eliminate our appliances. We don't use some of the watt guzzlers anyway- hair dryers, curling irons, coffee makers; but our water heater was old when we bought the house, so no telling it's exact age, and from the faded label on the side, uses a whopping 4,500 watts of electricity. Granted I'm a terrible laundress and only wash in cold water, we don't have an automatic dishwasher (well, sort of- my wonderful husband gets up from the dinner table and automatically does them), and we all take short showers in the morning, but DANG. So Mr. Water Heater is first on the appliance Hit List- my husband has been drooling over the tankless super-efficient ones at the Home Depot for several years anyway.

Our other appliances are not too bad. Our fridge and freezer are both 1/3 smaller than most folks' and under 5 years of age. Our little apartment sized dryer, bless it's heart, was a reject from the clinic I manage when they upgraded to a full sized model, but since it's smaller, uses less than half the watts of a full sized dryer. Our washer, handed down to me used when my 18 year old son was still in cloth diapers, will have to be replaced also, but not mainly as an electrical issue, but a water one- our plumber estimates it's using almost 50 gallons per load.

The kicker of course, is that these trusty old appliances are STILL WORKING. I guess there's something to be said for replacing them BEFORE they screech to a halt, but I'm still from the "You don't buy new, you make do" generation. Replacing our appliances with new efficient ones will shave another 35% from our usage, taking us down to half our current consumption without touching a solar panel, battery or inverter.

STEP THREE: we can address the solar installation in stages, starting with enough panels to produce about 1/2 our needs, during most months, and build up from there.

You can, if you are a do-it-yourselfer, climb-on-the-roofer, not-askeerd-of-high-voltager, put together your own solar system, buying piece by piece the panels, batteries, inverters and whatnots OR you can find a company who's been doing this for years and has pre-packaged units that are slightly altered according to situation, who come to your house and install the whole shebang (Howdy, come on in, I'll whip up a fresh batch of tea. Sweet or Unsweet?).

Now, since we already have electricity, courtesy of TXU Electric, a tie-in system just makes sense. If we have rain for a week like we did back in June and we deplete our stored power, the system will shift to TXU electric so seamlessly (supposedly) that only our computer will notice it. If we are making more than we can store, the surplus power gets washed back into the Grid and our meter runs backwards (I want to SEE that)!
There is a disconnect option, so anytime we want to, we can completely cut off from the Grid and be a freestanding entity.

Armed with my electric bill, the customer service number, and the righteous knowledge that it's federally mandated that power companies must buy back excess electricity produced, I bravely called TXU Customer Service. Note that I HAD been warned that the power company would not HAPPILY buy back electricity nor would they make it easy. After mucking through the swamp of "for my convenience" voice mail options and people who had no inkling of what I was talking about ("So why are you putting lights on the roof?"), I reached the executive offices and was told by Ms. Generic Phonevoice "Your call is VERY IMPORTANT to us. Please leave a message and we will return your call". Still waiting...

After chatting with Phil at Solar Installations in Dallas, who has been in the solar business for over 20 years, I was assured that he has installed systems for folks using our electric company, and after he educates them some, they have always gone ahead and installed a net meter.

Well, Class, what have we learned? We have learned something that our friends Homesteading in the Boonies already know- we need to THINK about where stuff comes from. We are so removed from the sources of everything, even those of us growing our own fruit and veggies (turn on the sprinkler and water comes out, cook and can on the stove, store in the freezer), raising our own livestock (electric fencing, lights for those early morning and winter evening feedings, tank heaters for the Snowbirds), and working those Homestead Crafts and Skills (power tools and tractors anyone?) need to sit up and take notice.

If we pay more attention to our consumption, and take steps to be responsible for our own power production, we will pay less to Reddy Kilowatt, and simultaneously pay into our children's' healthy future on a healthy planet.

Cutting the Utilical Cord Part 2
Evicting the Sewer Gators

Water. We turn on the tap, and there it is. But where did it come from? How has it been treated (or not)? And where does it go once we are done with it?

If you are like us, you are connected to a municipal water/sewer system that performs reasonably well. The water is supposedly drinkable, looks and smells pretty good, and none of the kids has sprouted a third eyeball (yet).

We have been questioning our particular municipality about several issues and between the unsatisfactory answers and the rising costs (water, sewer and garbage pickup in our little town costs between $50 and $75 per month); we are ready to chuck the whole system.

One of the issues is that our drinking water smells very chlorine-ish most of the time, accompanied by an alka selzer look and sound to it. I once cleaned my little boy's goldfish bowl and within 5 minutes, the fish were belly up. Good thing they were nondescript orange ones, easily and quickly replaced. My neighbor's son has actually been pelted by chlorine hail coming out of the shower. Our city water comes from a well, or several wells, they aren't very precise down at city hall. Now, our city only has but 745 folks in it, but that's gotta tax a well (or several wells).

We need a new source of water.

Our other issue is a murky sludge pit down at the corner of the property that smells suspiciously like sewerage. I call, I complain, the water dudes come out, dig a hole, stand in said hole smoking cigarettes, fill up the hole and declare it fixed.

We need a way to take care of our own wastewater.

Issue One-The three hurdles to water acquisition are-

-Finding your water source
-Storage of water
-Delivery of water to the household

The traditional way to take care of this is to call a well digger and pay him to drill a well somewhere in the area of 40-150' down (costs and depths will vary according to your location, around here it's about $15 per foot), and a septic guy and hand him around $5,000 to sink a 3,000-5,000 gallon holding tank and clay tile leach field that will take ALL the water from your house and infect it with the little bit from your toilets, rendering it all disgusting. There are several obvious problems with these two options.

Our underground water supply is being sucked dry from agriculture, manufacturing and urban/suburban sprawl. It will take between 2,000 and 5,000 years to replenish our aquifers once they run out, and that's a long time between showers. If drilling is out, that leaves us with standing groundwater (ponds, streams, rivers and lakes), springs, or rainwater catchment.

Most of North America's groundwater is still potable, unless directly downhill from a major contaminant (nuclear station, foundry, lots of moo cows). If you are lucky enough to have a natural body of water on your property, you have a "source and storage combo" and all you need is a delivery system which can be anything from a carried bucket to a sophisticated pumping system run by standard electric, wind generator or solar panels.

Another earthbound source of water is an underground spring. Some springs show only as little muddy patches surrounded by lots of water-loving plants- kind of a mini marsh.

Once you have determined that this stays marsh like all year, you most likely have a year-round spring and can develop it. Depending on your skills and money, this can be simply dug out, lined with rocks and fenced off, all the way to constructing a bona fide well house. This too is it's own storage "tank" so all that's needed is a delivery system.

And there's always rain. Catching rainwater leaves out the potentially contaminated groundwater middleman. Even in the driest spots in the US, if you are careful about collection and conservative about usage, rainwater can provide a lot of your household's needs. In cold climates, the precipitation will have to be siphoned into the house to avoid freezing. Collecting off of the roof of your house is the most obvious catchment- just be sure there's nothing toxic in your shingles. There are diverters made that dump the first rainwater from the roof, then spin to catch the rest of the water off of the rinsed surface. Rainwater can be caught in cement, wooden or plastic barrels or cisterns and there should be some sort of tight mesh cover to keep out skeeters, leaves and the occasional suicidal rodent.

Your delivery system can be buckets and forced child labor, hand pumps (personally, I loved the kitchen sink hand pump in my grandparents' summer cottage and I'll always remember my little brother pumping the outside pump and a frog falling out), electric pumps, wind generated pumps or solar pumps. The solar pumps must receive at least 4 hours of direct sun per day to be effective. More is better, of course. The average pumping system works best if located 200' or less from the house. You can purchase pressurized holding tanks so your pump doesn't run every time someone washes their hands.

Now that you have your water and have chosen a delivery system- what do you do with it once it's in your house?

There are roughly a bazillion different water Treatment and water Purifying gizmos being marketed. The first step is to have the water tested to see what nasties you need to eliminate, since different gizmos blast different things. You can have your water tested by your County Ag Extension (average cost $200), or you can purchase a kit from a private company like Suburban Water Testing (www.h2otest.com).

Most times, depending on your test results, you can get away with just filtering the water for everything but consumption.

A low tech but still effective way to kill living organisms in your water is to boil it for 10 minutes. This does not filter out harmful non-organic matter, however.

Filter systems do just that- filter out things like arsenic, mercury and lead, and although they do trap bacteria, they don't kill it. In fact, the filters are a wonderful breeding ground for bacteria. This results in water that may be more bacterial than it was raw (bad).

Reverse osmosis is also used to treat for toxic heavy metals, and it too lacks in the living organism destruction department.

Filtration and reverse osmosis are considered "treatments", boiling and steam sterilizing (distilling) are considered "purifications".

Steam sterilizers usually come with a filter attachment, covering most of the bases.

Included in the list of What's Nasty in the Water are
-Organic impurities like algae or sewerage. These will cause the water to stink and taste bad
-Inorganic impurities like sand, silt and salt. These cause turbidity- dirty looking water
-TDS (total dissolved solids), which will give the water that metallic taste, leave hard water scales in the shower, and include excess fluoride. Yes, you CAN have excess fluoride. I found this out in Wisconsin when we moved to the country and had well water. My daughter's teeth developed white streaks and I thought "Oh, sure. We move to the country to have a healthier life, and because the water isn't fluoridated, her teeth are suffering". Turns out the water naturally has too MUCH fluoride. In the municipal treatment process, this all gets taken out and then they add just a little back in. Your tax dollars at work.
-Toxic/heavy metals including lead, mercury and arsenic
-Toxic organic chemicals courtesy of the manufacturing industries to the tune of one billion pounds per year nationally
-VOC (volatile organic compounds), which are lightweight and evaporate

-Chlorine. Yes the same stuff used to make our drinking water safe will, when mixed with the right organic substances mutates into THM (trihalomethanes) linked to cancer, high blood pressure and chronic anemia
-Pesticides/herbicides (poison, no explanation necessary)
-Asbestos. Unbelievably, asbestos cement is the stuff water pipes were made of. Unbelievablier, over 200,000 miles of this still carries water to a lot of folks' kitchen sinks.
-Radionuclides including uranium and radium

Of course (hopefully) your water won't have ALL the above floating around in it, and testing it will determine the type of treatment/purifying your water needs to make it safe.

Issue Two- What to do with the water AFTER you use it. Obviously, the septic route is wasteful and expensive.

The water from sinks, showers, clothes and dishwashers is considered "grey" water- used, but not totally abused. There is no reason this can't be collected and diverted to your veggie garden. In fact, the bits of food, soap (safe, biodegradable soaps are available and are, I think, superior to the other stuff anyway and no more expensive), and teensie bits of skin cells from washing are good for your plants. The simple way is to run pipe directly to the garden using a soaker hose irrigation system. You can get as elaborate as your imagination or industriousness allows. I have plans for several "branches" of said pipes that I can alternate from veggies to flowers and back via the use of cut off/diverter valves.

Toilets produce "black" water. Black water treatment/ disposal is much more rigidly regulated by local municipalities and there are many many ways to go about this unpleasant but necessary chore. In fact, just the discussion of toilets merits it's own chapter in our quest for utility independence, therefore I won't be opening this "can" of worms (sorry) quite yet.

Better to leave ya'll clutching your magazine, banging on the door and hopping up and down. (smile)

Cutting the Utilical Cord Part 3- When the Going Gets Tough, Where Will the Tough Be Going?

No topic is more avoided, hotly debated, and the cause of downright obsessive behavior than excrement. From the moment of our birth, our mothers and other caregivers are creepily concerned with our toilet habits. They are told to count wet diapers to gauge hydration, warily eye the differences in poopage and are as loyal to brands of diapers as they are to their spouses.

And potty training? Don't get me started.

As grownups, of course, we no longer have these concerns.

Don't bet on it.

In the beginning, there were the bushes. You just picked a likely looking clump and there you had it; The Casual Bathroom.

Of course, if all your relatives used the same clump, things would soon pile up, so to speak.

Enter the outhouse. A pit is dug and a shelter constructed over it for privacy and protection from inclement weather Periodically, lime is added to aid in the breaking down of the waste. Once the pit is almost full, it's covered over with dirt, a new pit is dug, and the shelter moved on top of the new pit. It's simple and straightforward. Also stinky, full of bugs in the summer and freezing cold in the winter, plus it's a long walk (or sprint) in the middle of the night.

With the urbanization of humanity, came the desire to perform bodily functions in the comfort of your home. While chamber pots were easy and low-tech, there was a perceived need for something even easier, less odiferous and more hands-off.

The Father of the Modern Bathroom was Thomas Crapper. He is credited with the design of the first flush-type toilet, changing the way the world would "go" forever. For several generations, this has been the norm in all but the most remote areas of our country.

Hey, look! It's modern-day Homesteaders!

See how happy they are roaming their hard-won acreage!

Marveling at the wildlife and plant life!

Building their own little house, or just camping out until they can afford to build!

Planting a garden and tending it, reveling in the wonder of the seasons!

Hmmmm. They look a little uncomfortable.

Kinda hopping up and down with their faces all twisted up.

OH NO, WHERE WILL OUR HOMESTEADERS "GO"?

The phrase "Back to Nature" was never used in a more appropriate manner.

Of course the shrubberies are still there, as is the option of the pit toilet outhouse. But thanks to the Wonders of Modern Science, our Homesteaders have several other options.

The Composting Toilet-
A composting toilet consists of indoor parts that look a lot like a flush toilet except it looks like the tank is beneath instead of behind and there's a vent pipe going up through the roof. It's a lot like the toilets on airplanes or trains with the waterless bowl and flapper bottom. Your compost toilet must be several feet above ground level to accommodate the outside part, which is the composter itself. With an assortment of vents, fans, and hardworking microbes, the waste is turned into a small amount of pure compost

that empties from a tray. This type of toilet runs somewhere in the area of $1,200 (www.envirolet.com)

The Incinerating Toilet-
This one is totally cool. It requires no plumbing, venting or outside apparatus. It also looks pretty conventional. When it's time to use the toilet, you drop a paper liner in the bowl and go. At the press of a button, the paper and contained waste will drop into the bottom and be FRIED into a tiny pile of harmless ashes. My own personal misgivings about this come from having a 4 year old in the house. I'm not so concerned about HIS safety, as his TOYS' safety (let's see what happens to a matchbox car in the Inferno. Awesome! Now Teddy's turn) If you have no small children or have better control over yours than I do mine, and go shopping for this type of system, expect to spend about $1,700. (www.incineret.com)

But let's say our Homesteaders have no source of the electricity that both these options require.

And maybe, just maybe, they have better things to do with several thousand dollars than buy toilets. Fear not, for there is always

The Sawdust Toilet-
This is basically an outhouse in reverse. With a sawdust toilet, a 5-gallon bucket is fitted with a toilet seat and several inches of sawdust are placed in the bottom as a starting layer. Each time the toilet is used, more sawdust is added. This keeps the contents from attracting bugs and repelling humans. Once the bucket is filled, it's taken out to the compost bin, emptied and covered. It's recommended that the compost bin have 3 sections- 1 for fresh compost, 1 for last year's compost (to be used as needed) and 1 for surplus sawdust storage. Cost for your Sawdust toilet and compost bins- under $200.
(www.jenkinspublishing.com/sawdustoilet.html)

Of course, you need to check with your local Code Lords to see which option is open and legal for you to pursue, but certainly, all of the above make more sense than taking a small amount of waste, mixing it with mega gallons of clean water, and then trying to clean it all up. I mean, really, think about it.

We as Homesteaders take great pride in being responsible for everything that goes into our families. We need to be just as responsible in regards to what comes out of them.

For Sale By Owner- Needs A Little Work

The old house crouched in the weeds, summoning as much dignity as it could, missing parts of its roof, some walls, and some windows. Not quite level, layers of paint peeling off the warped siding, it was abandoned, deserted, unloved.

It had good roots, built in 1890 in a nice neighborhood in a growing city by a family who loved it for many years. Neighborhoods change, however, and families move on. It was turned into a boarding house for college students, and after a time, the lot it sat on was sold for parking. It became For Sale to be Moved.

In 1976 the house was dissected- it's top floor shaved off, dismantled and sold for scrap, the original gingerbread trim sold to renovate other vintage houses, and the main floor cut down the middle to facilitate the 20 mile move to it's new resting place- 4 acres in the woods on the edge of a little town.

The Unkind Fates weren't done with the house yet. After being reassembled and "updated" to '70's chic (shag carpeting, dark faux paneling, avocado green appliances) the new owners never moved into the house and it went through three different rent-to-own-ers, all of them having to be evicted for non-payment. Folks who are evicted do not take the best care of a place. It sat empty, quiet and alone for several years.

Meanwhile, a woman was slogging through her own journey. Although her history didn't reach quite back to 1890, she sure felt like it. On the tail of her second failed marriage, working two full time jobs to make ends meet, she had just moved out of the worst trailer park in Texas and into the home of friends, kind of a lateral move self-esteem-wise, but physically safer.

All her life, she'd wanted to redo an old house in the country, but though she'd owned two homes, neither had been the home of her dreams. Twice a day she drove past this house, just down the hill from her friends' house. She'd even toured it (easy because remember, it was missing doors and walls, you just walked in) and fantasized about what it once looked like and what it could be again.

Although the asking price was ridiculously low, it was still out of her reach. She was now seeing a Good man, and one day at lunch he asked her how low it would have to be for her to afford it. Out of the blue, she picked a number and they both laughed. When she got home that night, her friend said that the owners had called that day to tell them that they had lowered the price of the house to exactly the amount she'd come up with.

Well, she may have had a run of bad luck, but she still knew a Sign when she saw it.

The owners gave her 3 months to scrape together the tiny down payment and the house became hers.

OK- the mood has been set. Poor sad house. Poor sad woman. Sad woman finds Sad house. If you don't know by now that "she" is really "me", than you are sharp as a sack of wet mice. From here on in, the story will be written in the first person, because the other way is giving me a headache.

The first years were like primitive camping, only not as glamorous.

I closed on the house in December of '95. I didn't move in till April because it really was unlivable, even for me. All the initial work on and in the house was done by me and several good friends, mainly my neighbor, who gave me moral support and constantly reminded me that mere chicks can do most anything with the right attitude and access to really big power tools; and the man who is now my husband, who quietly surveyed the "Diamond in the Rough" and instead of running screaming the other direction like most sane folks would've done, just nodded and said "Lotta work". My nine-year-old son was too busy with the neighbor boys to care what his mom was doing, and my 14-year-old daughter announced,

"Mother, this is not a fixer upper. This is a burner downer".

The first order of business was to gut it down to the bones. The flooring was disgusting and the kitchen cabinets were unspeakably nasty. We ripped the carpets off the floors, dragged them outside and burned them. It took several burns to really kill them, and even now there are still some fragments poking through the weeds. The linoleum was pried up and broken off of the floors. Underneath all this mess were the original pine floors. Even though the house had been empty for several years, there was still food (or what used to be food) in the cabinets. There was not enough bleach in the universe to clean them up, so out came what were to be our three main tools for the next 7 years- pry bars, sledgehammers and a big ol' heapin' helpin' of EEEWWWWWWW. When we dragged the cabinets out to add to the burn pile, we brought along the avocado dishwasher, unopened. There was no way I was looking inside THAT.

I had no fridge at first, just a counter top model my mother-in-law loaned me. There was no stove, but I found I could cook just about anything between my Crockpot, toaster oven, electric griddle, and a propane camp stove.

There were several rooms on the back of the house that had been added after the move, and they had not been properly attached to the main structure, causing water to run down between the walls. They had to go. The most effective, enthusiastic and affordable wrecking crew is several preteens armed to the teeth with tools of de-struction. On a fine sunny Saturday morning my crew gazed at me through their safety goggles, clutching their sledgehammers in their work-gloved hands, a dusting of sugar donut fuel still on their faces, as I instructed them "Everything behind this point comes down". Tentatively, they tapped at the walls till I grabbed a sledgehammer and said "NO, like THIS", and slammed a gigantic hole in the wall. There was a moment's stunned silence, then mayhem. Within an hour, there was only a pile of refuse where the rooms had been, and one lad came up to me, still trembling with the excitement of pure positively directed violence. Grimy and sweaty, sledgehammer still in hand, he crowed, "This has been the best day of my life!"

There was no heat in the house, and even though I waited to move in till April, it was still darn cold. There was a spot in the back hall where a woodstove had been, but one of the evictees had taken it with him, and there's an under the floor furnace in the front of the house that a heating/ac installer had said IS usable. If we all want to die. I'd eat my breakfast cereal perched on the toilet because the bathroom was the only room I could get warm enough with a space heater. My kids came down for Easter and my daughter wrapped herself in her electric blanket and went through the house like a Cocoon with feet, trailing an extension cord. One day she proclaimed "Bad news Mom. It is warmer in the fridge than out here".

By fall, I had saved what I thought was enough money to install a gas line for a furnace. A plumber quoted me several thousand dollars to do the job. When my eyes glazed over and I started to sway, he told me I could borrow the tools I'd need if I wanted to do it myself. He dropped off a pipe threader and a pipe cutter and showed us how to use them. The pipe was delivered and we started to dig our trench- over 200' hand dug between the roots of 3 gigantic oaks to the house. Once at the house, we donned miner's hats, said prayers to the God of all Things Crawly and dove underneath. We installed t-joints anywhere we thought we might someday need one- at the fireplaces (I wasn't sure if I was going wood burning or gas), by the water heater (so I can replace the electric with gas when it finally dies), for the stove, and on to the back of the house where the furnace would sit. The same installer who had given me the dubious recommendation for the current furnace appeared with a furnace someone had replaced with a new one, fitted with a hood to blow forward, and installed it for free. I had heat.

The first winter I shared the house with a family of raccoons. This was not my idea, it was theirs. They moved into the attic and rearranged it to suit their tastes. There was a layer of blown in insulation up there that they took an especial dislike to and spent hours chucking it down through the hole in the living room ceiling. Every few days I'd find a massive pile of the stuff on the floor. There's an attic access door up high in the master bedroom wall and one morning as I was lying in bed the door slowly opened and a little pointed nose peeked out. He and I stared at each other for a minute, and then a little humanlike hand extended and quietly pulled the door shut. Summer in the attic must've gotten too warm, because they moved out and didn't come back.

The house is blessed (or cursed, depending on the season) with huge windows all around. Two feet wide by 8 feet tall sometimes doubled, bathing the house in natural light that streams in and reverberates off of the 12' ceilings. When the kitchen was "updated", they removed the windows to allow for the installation of traditional built-in counters and cabinets. A window that was 24" square was tucked over the sink. The tiny window, dark paneling, cheap cabinets and red brick patterned linoleum gave the kitchen a very cavelike feel. Ripping the cabinets out helped. Tearing up the linoleum helped. We had saved the windows from the rooms we tore down and we chose one with easily working ropes and pulleys, cleaned it up and commenced to cut a big hole in the wall that we hoped was window sized. In streamed the light, banishing the cave monsters.

The first summer, I allowed the kids to do their rooms. From choosing colors to measuring and figuring out how much paint they needed, this was THEIR deal.

My daughter's room is what used to be the dining room. Double windows, a transom window from her room to the hallway connecting it to the kitchen, wooden wainscoting, a chair rail all around and a door onto a tiny porch give it a lot of character. When we moved in this room was painted white with pepto bismal pink woodwork. She chose blue to replace the pink. The walls and ceiling are a light blue, almost white, and the woodwork just a shade darker. The wainscoting is sponge painted, as are the doors. Our neighbor found an old wrought iron light fixture at a garage sale, painted it white and rewired it for this elegant room. Her favorite art posters are wallpaper glued to the walls, framed with slivers of wallpaper borders. A rainforest wallpaper border above the chair rail, rag rugs, calico curtains and new quilt for her great-great- grandmother's bed completed the look. She sent out a declaration of independence from the rest of the house, as her room was too cool to coexist with the shabbiness around it.

My son's room is on the other side of the kitchen, what used to be the "keeping room" for putting up produce. The woodwork is not as fancy as the Main house, but it does have double windows and is attached to the sun porch. He chose green and a fish theme. We texture painted over the cheap paneling and it was too dark. In trying to come up with something a 9 year old could do, I hit on thinning a little pale green paint, putting it in a spray bottle and telling him to zap the walls. It has a nice spatter effect and lightened the walls. We stenciled fish on all the woodwork and realized that 2 of the 4 types of fish didn't have eyes (!). Off we went to the craft store, and many little googly eyes and dabs of hot glue later, all the fishies were able to see. Dark green plush carpet (remnant store, cut to size like a big area rug), undersea posters, whale wallpaper border and trout bedding finished it out.

The master bedroom was originally the den, with ceiling high built in bookcases and a fireplace. When the house was moved, the bricks were removed from the fireplaces/chimneys and they were not replaced. The fireplaces were still there, lovely old wooden mantels intact, but boarded up. The walls were as most of the rest-nasty dark fake paneling that had chunks broken out of it in places, warped in places, and thousands of staples and nails everywhere else. We wondered what was under all this nasty paneling, so we pried up a corner of it. We found very old wallpaper on top of cheesecloth on top of wood. Solid wood. Curious, we did the same thing in each room of the house. More wood. The house was solid wood, some so old and petrified that we couldn't drive a nail into it. Other spots were pocked by an old termite population, and still others were water damaged.

How to "fix" the walls on a shoestring budget? OK, who am I fooling? My budget was not shoestring; it was the Dust on a Bug's Shoestring. Enter my friend- fabric. The master bedroom was swathed in plain muslin, applied with finishing nails, topped with a fern border also nailed in place. This set off the dark woodwork. Since the room was once the library, it had no closet, but it did have an alcove. I found bed sheets in a pattern that I liked that were the perfect size for curtains (with the size of the windows, draperies would have been custom, read Expensive) and curtained off the alcove with the help of a spring type shower rod. Instant closet. Another trip to the remnant store scored a nice patterned Berber that we cut to fit.

The house has a main central hall and rooms opening into it on each side. Each side room opens into the room behind and in front of it also. When I purchased the house I had no worries or intentions of ever having to chase a toddler around the many circular patterns that can be run in here, but life is funny. Five years ago, when my other kids were 13 and 18 another child joined the family, born right here with two midwives in attendance. Trying to catch the little bugger takes a team of at least 2 adults-one to flush and one to catch.

The central hallway was painted gangrenous infection green over '50's institutional green wainscoting and woodwork. A single light bulb tried valiantly but unsuccessfully to light it. It took 3 coats of light peach paint and another rummage sale light fixture (a magnificent wrought iron whimsy of palm leaves and blossoms) to transform it into an inviting entryway. The floor in the hall, front to back, was particleboard. It had deteriorated over the years and was not in any condition to lay the tile I'd like eventually, so back to the remnant store we went for simple white roll linoleum.

This is as good a point as any to remark that I don't like white walls. My goal for my house was to have every room a different color. Also, there is something completely freeing about working with a house in this state of disrepair. You can try whatever you want to, and no matter how dismal the results are, it will still be an improvement.

Double French doors open into the back hall, which serves as the utility/sewing room. It was grey with a plywood ceiling. I painted it lavender with iris and dragonfly wallpaper and hot glued lavender pinstripe fabric (OK, bed sheets) to the ceiling. Important scientific observation- when using hot glue on the ceiling, gravity is NOT your friend. And when a glop of the molten glue does fall on your hand, your first inclination is to quick wipe it off with your OTHER hand, giving you double burns to enjoy. Someday this will be a metal ceiling, but many of the initial projects were necessarily cost-effective "first wave" decorating. Surprisingly, a number of these projects turned out so well, I don't want what I originally thought I did. A roll down shade hides the furnace from view, and rolls up to service it.

The kitchen was one of the rooms that had undamaged walls under the paneling, wallpaper and cheesecloth, so these were painted pale yellow. There are 3 doors into the kitchen- one from the back hall, one from my daughter's room and one to my son's room. One of these retained the original transom window, but the other two had been gleaned and sold, the holes badly patched. Someday, I hope to find matching transoms, but for now, they are covered with "mirror windows" purchased from the local home improvement center. When the counters were ripped out, it left me sinkless, and I purchased a large utility sink that I love for roughly 1/4 the cost of the cheapest "kitchen" sink. I can wash lots of produce and small dogs (not at the same time), and it hides a fair amount of dishes. I have taken the art-on-the-fridge idea to the extreme and framed toddler masterpieces with frames from the dollar store. They cover the walls almost to the 12' ceiling.

The bathroom contained what was indisputably the most valuable item in the house- a metal claw footed tub. As far as I can tell, the only reason they didn't sell it was because they actually built the bathroom around the tub, and it won't fit through the door. Unfortunately, it had been painted pink. Then brown. It took several coats of white to get it back. A new pedestal sink, pale pink paint to cover the dark brown (like all the dark brown paneling hadn't been enough), and a flock of flamingos and the bathroom was good to go.

We reached a point where we could tackle the "Big Stuff", projects we didn't have the skills or youth to do. The day they shingled the roof was a banner day. For six months after the roof was put on, the first thought in my head when it clouded up was "Are the buckets empty and in the right spots?" Then I'd smile. If I was at home, I'd stand under where we used to be roofless and listen to the rain, feeling all warm and fuzzy inside.

With the new roof on, we could finally do the living room. Time had not been kind to the living room. There were gaping holes in the ceiling, the walls were water damaged and so was the floor. The living room is another place I'd like a pressed tin ceiling, but for now it's white metal ridged siding, and it looks pretty slick. My husband asked what color the woodwork was going to be and I told him without hesitation Red. Red? Red. He just shook his head and walked away. I painted the woodwork before doing the walls, so was painting next to the nasty dark paneling, and of course, when the paint was wet, it was shiny. Shiny Fire Engine Red. Bravely I painted on, and the finished product is striking and dramatic. Fabric was brought into play again for the walls. I found a pattern of tiny floral calico in multi colors and ordered 8 bolts. Seen from a distance of a few feet, it looks muted, not busy. It's a lovely counterpoint for the Victorian Red woodwork. Remnant store again (they love me there) for more Berber carpet, but hmmm- it's 12' wide and the room is 16'. Patterned runners along each side form a border.

There was a large porch off of the living room that had fallen down with the other rooms we dismantled. The foundation beams for this porch were still there, and, in fact were proving to be all but impossible to pry off. It was therefore decided to make half into a deck off the living room and the other half a badly needed second bathroom that would open onto the back hall. The one wall of the bathroom was in fact the outside of the living room wall, so, solid wood. Our contractor picked out lovely pine planks to make the other walls and I satin polyurethaned them and the ceiling (another project where gravity is not your friend). The first time my older son saw the new bathroom he announced "Smells like Canada". Whatever that means.

The last room to be done was the sun porch off the boys' room. I was officially out of colors to choose from, and the walls were in good enough shape to hold wallpaper, so the room became plaid. When we opened the door to our little son's new playroom, he exclaimed, "I love it. It's my tree house!" And you know, with the windows all around and the forest pressing in, it truly is.

Siding the house was a hard decision. I really wanted to save the original wood siding, but was given the news by several painting contractors that to repair and replace and THEN paint would be roughly three times as costly as vinyl siding. My contractor (who loves old houses) pointed out that siding has come a long way in the last few years and there are different widths and styles you can choose from. We chose a narrow width, like the original, and even found vinyl medallions and fancy trim for over the windows and doors similar to what was sold off of the house before it was moved. There are even vinyl "fish scales" for on the peaks. All in all, after the siding was done, the house looked much more from it's own period than it had in years. After the siding was complete, one neighbor called to complain that now his property taxes would go up (grin), and another still brings people down the road to show them what we've done to the house.

Less glamorous projects included insulation in the attic, the walls and under the house (there had been NONE), installing ductwork and hooking up the furnace to it (heat in every room, all the time), and moving the circuit box indoors (I kinda miss standing in the dark, in the rain, in a puddle, flipping circuits) and adding a few new ones. The house had 8 circuits when we moved in, no 220. In the kitchen, if we were making Sunday breakfast, we could make toast, and eggs, but if we wanted the coffee maker on, we'd have to turn the lights off. Now we have over 30 circuits, and don't use but 1/2 of them. There's 220 if we need it.

We chose to have the windows reglazed rather than replaced. It's not energy efficient, especially given the size and number of the windows, and it was costly, but I just couldn't part with the old, lovely wavy glass. When I first moved into the house and it was room after room floor to ceiling bleakness and despair, I would lie in bed and look out the windows at the oak trees and marvel at how beautiful they looked through that glass.

The ultimate finishing touch was getting the fireplaces back in working order. The first night with a fire was glorious. There is nothing more decadent than a fire in the fireplace in your BEDROOM, cocoa on the bedside table, good book in hand, snuggled under quilts with dogs and family all contentedly snoring next to you.

Oh, there are still lots of things that need doing, or re-doing. A house is like your life, a constant work in progress. The important thing is that after a long hard journey, a sad tired woman found a sad tired house and together, with a lot of help and a lot of hard work, they are Home.

Postscript- The story you have just finished is an unabashed love story to my house. Even though the winds of change may blow me elsewhere, and onto new challenges, this house will be forever in my heart as the old house in the country that I finally had the privilege to restore. In bringing this house back to life, so my own life was healed and restored.

Livestock Guardian Dogs- JUST LIKE LASSIE- ONLY BETTER

When I had my dairy goats in Wisconsin, nothing bothered them and they lived happily and without a care in the world.

So when I got my land in Texas, I confidently fenced off an area, put up a little shelter, and installed two lovely Nubian doelings- China and Marigold, both pregnant.

One cold winter night, with the sleet blowing horizontally across the fields, I did not hear the goats calling me when I got home from work. I grabbed a flashlight and told my husband to stay at the house (city boy, with a very soft spot for the goats). The flickering beam of the flashlight confirmed my fears. The fence had been dug under by dogs and my beautiful goats lay dead, marred only by the gaping holes in their throats.

It was over a year before I could talk my husband into trying again.

The new goats- Alice and Trixie, were put into a different pen, adjoining the back porch. Whenever we were gone, or at night, they were locked up onto the porch. They found this to be really really boring (even for goats) and were not even remotely potty trained, making the porch toxic and stinky in short order, even though we'd bedded the whole thing with straw.

My search began for an LGD- Livestock Guardian Dog.

LGD's are dogs that are not herders, nor are they attack dogs. They are exactly what they are called- "Guardians". Their job is to live with the stock and make sure nothing gets in to hurt, steal, or eat it. Their first line of defense is just their size; they are enormous. If size and a menacing bark do not deter, they will place themselves between their charges and perceived danger. If all else fails, they will resort to violence, and woe to anyone on the receiving end of over 100 pounds of angry dog.

In this country we see mainly three breeds of LGD's- Komondor (Komondorok plural), Anatolian Shepherds, and Great Pyrenees (Pyrs).

Komondorok have white coats that grow in cords, like dreadlocks. They are cautious by nature, and tend to bond to only one person or immediate family, and are creepily formidable stalking a stranger. The Komondor Club of America stresses the importance of obedience training and socialization of the young puppy to help assure that your adult dog will be a stable member of society. These dogs are very intelligent and tend to think for themselves, so if you fail to establish your role as "head dog", your Komondor will happily assume he's in charge. The coat requires a lot of care, and when they get wet, they stay wet. Really. For weeks. I would be skeptical of how well they fare in a southern summer, but I have seen some here in Texas, so I guess they do all right.

Anatolian Shepherds (sometimes called Akbash dogs) are also generally cautious, with the Anatolian Sheperd Club giving the same advice about socialization and training as the Komondor club, but there are exceptions to every rule. The Austin Zoo has one who sleeps on the porch to the gift shop like a giant Welcome Mat that you have to take a BIG step over. Their coat is more like a lab or German shepherd, short and thick, and they come in various shades of grays and browns.

My personal experience is with Pyrs. I chose this breed for a number of reasons- they are the most friendly to strangers (anyone is calmly welcomed unless proven untrustworthy), their fluffy white coat sheds nicely into a summer coat with a minimum of brushing, and most importantly, because I got one for free.

Galut was the one remaining pup from a litter of 10, and her mother was frankly tired of motherhood. In a fit of annoyance, perhaps after hours of her puppy yapping nonstop into her ear while she was trying to watch her stories, Galut's mother grabbed her by the scruff and shook her, giving her a nice puncture wound. (I have honestly felt the same way about my own offspring on more than one occasion). Her owners just didn't want the hassle of treating it, and "poof", I had my LGD. Galut was 10 weeks old and over 25 pounds when she came home.

There are various thoughts on the proper training of these dogs. Some say they can't be proper guardians if they are treated as pets, and advocate tossing them in with the livestock and having no contact with them whatever- no petting, nothing. Although Galut went to live with the goats, not in the house, we have always made a big deal out of her, petting, baby talk, the whole nine yards, and she guards just fine.

They DO make good housedogs, and in fact the next time we are in the market for a housedog, a Pyr will be what I look for. In the absence of livestock to guard, they become excellent babysitters. I've heard of more than one Pyr pushing toddlers away from danger, and they not only tolerate small fry (goat kids OR human kids) crawling all over them, they adore it.

Even as a puppy, Galut never jumped up on us, and if I need to catch her and she's being playfully (but annoyingly) evasive, I send my 5 year old in after her. He just grabs her collar and brings her to me- 45-pound boy leading 110-pound dog.

Most trainers will tell you not to trust the dogs around newborn livestock till the dogs are over 2 years old, and I have to agree. For the first two springs, I tied Galut in a corner of the goat pen with a 20' chain till the babies were several weeks old. She was just too much of a puppy herself. She was so thrilled with the new playmates she'd grab them by the leg, hold them down with a giant paw and lick them till they almost passed out. Just like magic, the spring she turned 2 the over-exuberant teenaged puppy became a calm, benevolent matron.

I do have trouble when a baby goat imprints on her instead of its' mother. Sometimes it takes the better part of a week to convince the little one that cozy as Galut is, lunch comes from Mother.

With their size, you would expect LGD's to eat you out of house and home. When an LGD is working on a large ranch, in remote areas, the Gravy Train is scarce or non-existent, and these dogs have been bred accordingly. I feed Galut a 1# coffee can of mid-quality dry food twice a day, and to be honest, the goats eat about 1/2 of that before she loses patience with them and scatters them with a giant WOOF. A friend of mine has to feed her dog away from the goats, because her goats are not impressed with her dog's WOOF and ignore him. It is indicative of these animals' temperaments that they will go hungry before hurting one of their charges.

LGD's can be found through online clubs, word of mouth, or newspaper ads. Unless you are interested in dog shows, registration is not important. As with all big breeds, hip dysplasia is a concern, and I would take it as a very good sign if a breeder had his/her dogs x-rayed to check for soundness, since dysplasia is hereditary and a dysplastic dog can't do a very good job of guarding, and will have a shortened lifespan.

It is important to get a puppy and raise it up with your stock, or a young dog who has been raised with stock. Our first "freebie" Pyr was an adult stray and she'd obviously never seen goats. She wanted to chase them, plain and simple, and promptly moved on to a home with 2 old ladies to care for and who love her right back.

A lot of folks let their LGD have free run of their property. This is fine if you have ALOT of property. Your LGD will decide how far his/her territory goes, and your neighbors may not appreciate the big doggie that keeps pushing THEIR kids back into YOUR yard. Galut lives in the goat pen with the goats, and once when a coyote decided my chickens were a daily-special buffet, I turned her loose in the horse pen (mostly heavily wooded) for a few days to convince the coyote to move along.

Prices are hugely variable. You can pay up to a grand (or more) for a puppy with a fancy-shmancy pedigree if you want a show dog. For a well-bred LGD out of working parents expect to pay from $150 to $500. Every once in a while, if you keep your ears open, make your desires known and have patience, you will luck into one like I did.

Whether your LGD's charges are goats or toddlers and the predators are coyotes or burglars, these dogs will spend their lives keeping their family safe. When I have Galut filling the entire backseat of my car for a trip to the Vet, I look into those calm big brown eyes gazing over my shoulder. Even though she has never growled at anyone, I know that she would not hesitate to protect me.

It's a good feeling.

Dairy Goats- Anchoring Your Homestead with Personality and Ice cream

You've got your veggie gardens planted and your free-range chickens are happily scratching around eating their own weight in bugs and laying beautiful eggs for you every day. This Homesteading stuff isn't so hard (self-satisfied smirk)

In fact, it's the most natural thing in the world to take it another step, fence in that yard, put up a shed and go shopping for The Dairy Goat.

The first thing to consider is that goats are herd animals and if you get one, it WILL get out of the pen trying to find company. I recommend a minimum of 2 goats.

Your fence will need to be goat proof, and unfortunately, they haven't invented one of those yet. Wood fences are sturdy, but baby goats can slip out and coyotes can slip in. Wire fences can/will be bent over by your goats standing up on them reaching for whatever tiny leaf may be on the other side that looks more appealing than the million leaves on the inside. Barbed wire is just a nightmare waiting to happen. Electric will be bumped into systematically (accompanied by goat curses) till it breaks. The most effective goat fence I've found is the 16' cattle panels with the graduated spacing- narrower on the bottom than the top. These are non-bendable, quick to go up, and the only drawback is that if your goats have horns, they can get their heads stuck in the upper spaces if they are not careful/smart, so plan on your goats getting stuck now and again.

Goats must have shelter. The worst fate in the world to a goat is to be wet. If it's raining and the food is outside, they won't eat. A three-sided shed with the open end facing south is perfect for them.

Now just add "goats".

This can involve months of research into different breeds and bloodlines, contacting a breeder, waiting for a baby, taking delivery of said baby, raising that baby to adulthood, and doing MORE research to find the right Billy for your precious nanny, sometimes carrying her far afield for the perfect match.

Or, you can answer the ad in the Thrifty Nickel that reads, "Free Goat, heavy bred".

There are advantages and disadvantages to both strategies. If you are interested in breeding show goats and getting top dollar for babies- go with the first scenario. If you just want yard goats for personal use and pleasure, the second route is fine. After years of being in the world of "pedigreed" animals, I've come to the conclusion that a good crossbred anything is just as serviceable as the purebreds, and though my goat herd is currently all purebred Nubians, they are not registered, and when I find a buck to cross back to my buck's daughters, it most likely will not be a Nubian.

Of utmost importance, for the small homesteader is the health history of your goats. Have they been tested for TB (or come from a TB-free herd)?

CAE is common in some areas- and though the milk is fine for human consumption, you must pasteurize it before feeding to any goat babies or they may die. Any carriers of CAE can develop life-threatening arthritis.

All that said- you have your pen, your shelter, your goats, and their brand new kids.

Now what?

You need to decide if you will bottle raise those babies, or let mom do it. Again, it's purely personal- there is no right or wrong answer.

Bottle raising will give you goats so tame they will follow you through fire (just don't ask them to follow you through water). It is time-intensive as those babies are just that- babies who will need a bottle every 6 hours for the first few weeks. Add to that milking twice daily to get those bottles and you have a very busy schedule for a while. Of course there is NOTHING in the world cuter than a baby goat, so to most folks it's a small price to pay. This is also the way to go if you are planning on a larger-scale milk usage (commercial soap making for example) where you need your girls producing at full capacity for an extended period of time. (9 to 10 months).

Letting your mother goat raise her babies is much less time consuming, with a corresponding lower production. For my first years as a goat keeper, I would leave the babies with their mothers and milk twice a day. Sometimes I'd get a lot of milk, sometimes not a drop, depending on when the babies last ate. I'd wean the babies at 3 months, and continue milking twice daily. My goats would produce milk for about 6 months.

In my old age and slothfulness, now I totally ignore mother and babies for 3 months, then wean the babies and start to milk in the mornings only. A lot of this has to do with being in Texas as opposed to Wisconsin. Down here it's just too dang hot to be up under a goat in the heat of the day at 5 or 6pm. My girls produce milk for about 3 months. Since they are bred randomly year-round, I usually have someone in milk, and since they are pregnant for 5 months, that gives them a few months rest before more babies hit the ground.

There are people who will tell you that if you let the mothers raise the babies you will have a whole herd of goats wild as deer. This is partly true. My goats who are not bottle-fed are curious, but not pushy. They are harder to catch, but once caught generally give up and stand there instead of trying to run you down. As a rule, I like them better to work around on a daily basis. I have noticed very distinct differences in my bloodlines- Alice was bottle-fed and so is tame but all her non-bottle-fed babies are wild. Wilma was bottle-fed and so is tame but her non-bottle-fed babies are almost as tame as she is. I am concentrating on keeping more of Wilma's babies and less of Alice's (duh).

Feeding your goats properly is also of paramount importance if you will be drinking the milk. Anything that goes into your goat will flavor the milk. Period. Therefore, the more "bland" a diet your goat receives, the less of a "tang" the milk will have. Bland does NOT mean low nutrition. Your goat needs enough protein and fat to produce milk on an ongoing basis. A good NON medicated (unless you require daily worming) goat food (I feed an All purpose Livestock pellet) along with some sweet feed (9%) along with really high quality hay twice daily is a must.

Man, all that research and hard work to get your goats and their babies here has made you thirsty.

Got milk?

In the movies and the pictures in homesteading books, the Goat herder strolls into the milk house early in the morning; birds singing, sun just peeking over the horizon. She is carrying her milk stool and her milking bucket. At the quaint Dutch door of the immaculate barn, she calls her goat, who comes daintily dancing into the barn to the sound of distant bells ringing. A rosy glow infuses the milk house as the Goat herder gently places her stool next to the goat, who stands still as carved granite with a little goat smile on her face. The milk house is filled with the sound of warm fresh milk hissing rhythmically into the bucket. After a few peaceful minutes, the Goat herder lifts the bucket and pats the goat on the side. The goat gives an affectionate little "mmmaaa", and dances back out the door, which is quietly shut by clean little mice who wear tiny t-shirts (like on Cinderella).

This is an accurate portrayal, with the exception of the birds, sun, bells, glow, peace, and smiling well-behaved goat. The little mice really exist, or at least you will be positive that you see them as you careen out of the barn, covered in sweat and mosquito bites, hay in your hair, hair in your milk, milk most everywhere but the bucket, and the sound of laughter (the goat's) ringing in your ears.

Actually, these are both correct, depending on the day.

The first thing to learn is that goats are particular. They only like ONE person milking them, always and forever. I don't care if your son/daughter/husband feeds the goats every day, if you are the one milking, anyone else will be in for a Goat Rodeo lasting much more than 8 seconds, and resulting in at least as much bruising on the part of the human. This is something you need to be prepared for too, until you and your goat have an "understanding".

This Understanding must be reached every year when you start to milk. Since we are humans, equipped with large brains and opposable thumbs, we have the power of superior thought processes and leverage tools on our side. Thus the playing field is made somewhat more even.

To milk a goat, you need somewhere secure and clean to do the actual milking. This can be as elaborate as a separate "milk house" with little stanchions that hold the goat's head secure while you milk, to just tying the goat into a corner and kneeling next to her (what I do).

You need something to wash the udder with (all-natural "wet ones" are fine, or you can buy Udder Wipes from a milk supply place), and something to milk into (a large pot is fine. I splurged 2 years ago and got a lovely stainless steel bucket)

You will need your equipment set up for straining the milk (a metal colander lined with a Bounty paper towel- it MUST be Bounty- everything else will not drain fast enough and you will have a big mess, or a milk strainer from the afore mentioned goat supply place) a metal or glass bowl big enough to hold your strainer, container for milk, and pasteurizer, if you will be pasteurizing.

You will need a feed bucket and roughly 50# of sweet feed, for currency.

Until you and your goat have an "understanding", you will need the help of the biggest and most patient family member you have.

Have all your equipment clean and in place, including washing your hands well, gird your loins (not kidding) and proceed with your backup muscle and a bucket of sweet feed to the goat pen.

Since most goats are chowhounds, getting the goat to the tie-up is not a problem. Fighting your way through ALL the goats eager for a snack of sweet feed and getting only one goat is your first chore. Your clean hands are now dirty.

Once your goat is tied and eating happily, wash her udder. This may or may not be problematic. Most goats don't care. Some will be offended by the invasion of personal space and handily kick the wipe from your hands, never missing a beat in chewing the grain. Repeat till the goat's udder is at least as clean as your hands.

Here's where your Muscle comes in.

With one hand on the bucket (for quickly yanking out from under the goat), place the bucket under the goat and start milking. Several things can happen here.

a) Your goat will continue to eat, making no nevermind to you. If this is the case, say a silent prayer of thanks, try to keep the tears of joy from getting into the milk, but milk one handed for the first few times to make sure the goat is not lulling you into a false sense of security, only to neatly stomp her foot into your almost-full bucket. (Again, not missing any food)
b) Your goat will kick slightly, but settle down after a stern word or two. I still milk one-handed for a bit, just to make sure.
c) Your goat responds by wildly jerking her head up with a look of horrified indignance, rolls her eyeballs, sends the bucket flying across the barn with a swift kick, and swing smartly around, knocking you to the ground.

MOST of the time, you will be looking at "b", and the mere presence of an extra person is enough to convince a wise goat that she is indeed outnumbered and eating the sweet feed is payment enough for your stealing her milk.

If you are faced with a "c" situation, this just takes a little longer to resolve. Shorten the lead rope, and have your helper hold the goat's hindquarters against the wall while you milk. In some cases, I have had goats so wildly opposed to being milked, that they fight both of us. The important thing with goats (as with horses and children) is that you end all encounters on a good note. I have even cringed and milked really wild goats onto the ground, avoiding the bucket till they settle down some, just so they know that they WILL be milked, and it will NOT kill them (or me). Food is always there, and I always tell them how good they are and thank them when finished, but they ARE milked. I've not had one go longer than a week before settling down to eating as soon as I tie them, and ignoring me while milking.

Milking technique is important. The number one mistake I see people make is PULLING on the teats. You do NOT pull on the teats. You gently squeeze the teats just enough to get the milk, keeping your hand snug against the udder. Watch your wrists. They should not move. Rough milking causes mastitis, flakes in the milk, blood in the milk, and makes for a very crabby goat (understandably, think about it). Once the milk flow lessens, gently rub the whole udder, and then milk again, until you are not getting hardly any. You will not get ALL the milk, but you can get most of it. Milk is produced in a "supply and demand" fashion, so the more milk you take, the more she will make (assuming her diet is what it should be).

Once you and your goat have a routine, the entire milking process-from tying the goat to straining the milk, should take about 15 minutes. Actual milking time will be about 5 minutes per goat.

Your milk should be strained and refrigerated (or pasteurized and then refrigerated) immediately upon finishing milking and washing your hands. All equipment should be washed and dried and put up for the next milking. Leaving wash-up for later will cause milk "residue" to form on your equipment (yicky).

I once described the processes involved in milking to my banker at his request. He looked at me quizzically for a moment, and then said, "You know they SELL milk at the grocery store".

You either Get It, or you don't.

We who are doing "all this mess" are NOT crazy. We are feeding our families (at least partly) with good healthy food that we ourselves have produced.

We have veggie gardens for veggies.
We have chickens for eggs, meat, garden fertilizer and bug control.
We have dairy goats for milk, cheese, ice cream, yogurt, soap, lotion, meat and fertilizer.
It's all a Circle of Life thing, and we are a part of it, not mere consumers or spectators.

On a steamy summer morning, with the flies already biting, the sweat pouring down your nose, your goat clearly not amused, and visions of row upon row of chilled milk gallons at the air-conditioned Walmart, it can be hard.

But on a brisk pre-dawn winter morning, with your goat happily munching and your ear resting against her warm furry side, it's so quiet you can hear her tummy gurgling. You glance up at your home, one light on in the kitchen. Your family is inside, still sleeping or just waking up. You can smell the coffee over the good smell of clean healthy livestock and hay.

And the little mice in t-shirts smile and wink.

Using a Midwife- The Ultimate Do It Yourself Project

***Warning- this article contains some explicit references to childbirth. If you are the least bit woozy at the thought of this, you should probably re-think parenthood anyway.

I have three wonderful children.

When I was very young and newly married, I became a mother for the first time. My OBGYN was a very strict, humorless woman, who had delivered thousands of babies including my husband and myself. In her opinion, giving birth was a medical condition, and you listened to the Doctor with no questions asked.

After attending a few hospital-run 'Natural' Childbirth classes, I decided that
a) I was not attending any MORE hospital-run 'Natural' Childbirth classes, as they frankly made me want to hurl and
b) Drugs were a good thing. I told my OBGYN to empty her black case; I wanted at least 2 of everything, preferably washed down with some stiff spirits.

Due to some minor medical difficulties, however, when my lovely Erika made her debut I did not get my drugs, was bossed around and terrorized by the hospital staff and endured 12 hours of unwanted natural childbirth. After the fact, I was grateful for the natural childbirth part, since immediately afterward I felt wonderful and was ready to walk out of there with my new daughter. Because this was back in the "old days", they insisted that I remain a guest of the hospital for 3 days. The woman in the next bed had had a c-section and received all the drugs I thought I wanted. She spent the first 24 hours of motherhood sick as a dog.

Lesson #1- Drugs are not as great as they are cracked up to be.

Five and a half years later found me back in the same hospital for the arrival of David, who appeared after less than six hours of labor. This time my OBGYN was a wonderful man whose office walls were literally lined with photos of 'his' babies and who was of the opinion that birth is natural and wonderful and that his role was basically to be on hand just in case. Also to catch if the daddy passed out. He firmly believed that hospitals are the worst place in the world to have babies because they are full of germs. Unfortunately, Wisconsin was a state that was keeping its residents safe by making home births illegal, so the hospital was our only option. This time I was ready for the de-personalizing that every birth mom goes through from the hospital staff and with the blessing of my Doctor was much more vocal and adamant about what I would and would not endure at their hands to make THEIR jobs easier. After Erika, I knew I could have this baby without drugs and didn't request any. Insurance attitudes had also changed and they started a timer the second that baby took his first blink and escorted me out the door 24 hours later.

Lesson #2- hospitals are mostly superfluous to the birth event

Fast-forward 14 years.
Different state- Texas.
Different husband- one with no children, and what a shame is THAT?
Different circumstances- no insurance.

My interest in midwives and homebirth that my last OBGYN had sparked became suddenly extremely relevant upon learning at age 39 and 10 months that I was to become a mother again. Added to the above lessons learned early in life and my gut feeling that giving birth at home was just a 'righter' way to go about this, was the financial aspect- a hospital birth at right around $20,000 compared to homebirth of $1,200. Yes, the comma IS in the right spot and no I DIDN'T forget a few zeroes.

Enter Thalia; professional midwife, tireless coach, and dear friend. On our first visit, we went over my history. Given that I had given birth twice naturally with no major complications, she saw no need for alarm. Because I was over the age of 35 (read "High Risk Birthmother" to the medical community), she gave us the option of going to an OBGYN she worked with for an ultrasound or amniocentesis if we desired, and we declined. She told us we could deliver either at her birth center or at home if we lived within a 30-minute drive of a medical facility, and we do.

Midwives follow much the same procedure as an OBGYN with regard to scheduled appointments. They have the same schedule, they test for the same things using the same lab tests, and they monitor the baby's growth in the same ways. The difference is in the presentation. Their offices resemble (or truly are) their homes. The exam table is a real bed complete with comforter and pillow. There's not a stirrup, 2-year-old magazine or paper gown in sight. There is no waiting room full of other pregnant women. When you have an appointment, you are the patient. Period. The entire pregnancy is treated not as some deviant medical condition, but as a personal wonderment to be nourished and celebrated. What a concept.

Near the end of pregnancy, we gathered together supplies from a list provided and prepared for our birth. These items were readily available at the local grocery and drug stores.

We were encouraged to take home and watch a video of an actual home birth, which I slipped into the VCR with much trepidation (the video of an actual hospital birth is what sent me over the edge years before). I needn’t have worried. Instead of the brightly lit, fast paced, sterile delivery room full of serious brisk hospital staff who seemed to consider the birthing mother as an inconvenience to be tolerated was several hours of a family at home. The mother-to-be spent a lot of time in her rocking chair, reading to her other children, and walking with her husband. She drank some tea. Eventually she went to bed and proceeded to have her baby.

Here's why it was so important to see this after having 2 hospital births.

Doctors are trained to see everything in the Worst Case Scenario. When you have a hospital birth you may not walk around- you must be hooked up to the baby monitor. You may not eat or drink-you need an empty stomach in case they have to do a c-section. And once that little person hits the birth canal, look out- the hospital staff WILL deliver him/her within minutes, whether you and the baby are ready or not.

More and more it seems that Doctors also are performing c-sections or inducing labor for 'over term' pregnancies and even (I think shamefully) inducing so a woman will deliver to suit his or her schedule. Many of these 'over term' babies need to stay in the hospital or be treated for things that have traditionally been Preemie Problems. Obviously they weren't 'done' at all.

Midwives are trained to see pregnancy and birth as something women were designed to do (radical, I know) by Someone much smarter than any Doctor, and that MOST of the time, things go just as they should. They are there to help, but not run the show. And in the natural scheme of things, that means the birthmother can do whatever she wants to do and the baby shows up when good and ready, which is sometimes a LOT longer than any medical staff can wait around for.

The birthmother in the video labored longer, but much less frantically than the hospital mother, and the whole thing was actually peaceful and made me feel all warm and fuzzy inside instead of queasy and nauseated.

The reason that was so important for me to see is that Master Alec lollygagged around in the birth canal for over 30 minutes (after 14 hours of pre-game show) before finally deciding to grace us with his presence. Thalia assured me that this gave me time to adequately stretch (midwives do not do episiotomies) and not to take it personally, although sometimes I wonder...

But I've jumped ahead to the last page.

Our homebirth was just about the hardest and best thing we've ever done.

Thalia and her partner Linda arrived at our home just before midnight, after I'd been in mild labor for some hours. They encouraged me to walk, eat, and drink to keep up my strength. Once I was in labor I informed Ward that he was not to let go of my hand.

Ever.

And he didn't.

Our original plan was for Ward to catch the baby, but even with his really long arms, that was not going to happen with him holding my hand.

I will admit that about 20 minutes before the birth, I just flat shut down. I was tired. More tired than I'd ever been in my life. I decided that I couldn't do it, and made that fact abundantly clear to all on hand. Once I thought it through, though, I realized that if I trundled out to the car for the trip to the hospital, I'd most likely have the baby on the way. And if I DID make it to the hospital, there I'd be back in the very environment I had wanted to avoid. Armed with that knowledge, I first took a little nap (yes you can too nap if you are tired enough), and then with a final round of cheerleading from Ward and the midwives, Thalia delivered Alec at around 5am.

He did not cry. It was warm and dimly lit in our bedroom. No one was hurried or loud (except me, but that was before he arrived). Since we hadn't had an ultrasound, we didn't know until delivery whether we were having a boy or a girl, and I was so exhausted and happy to see the little critter, I forgot to even check.

Immediately after the birth, Thalia did all the state-required measurements and testing, but no eye drops. She uses a cloth sling to weigh babies in, not a cold metal tray that they roll around on, feeling like they are going to fall.

Once it was clear that all was well, the midwives packed up and left. Ward made us breakfast, and we all went back to bed.

Included in our fee were 2, count them, 2 home visits from our midwife after the birth- one at about a week and one at 6 weeks.

Homebirth may be right for you if-
-You are healthy and have no medical history that would preclude it
-You have a deep desire to keep pregnancy and birth a personal miracle rather than a medical condition
-You can get your brain around the concept of childbirth without so much as an aspirin (trust me on this, as I am a Bonified Weenie when it comes to pain-if *I* can do it, anyone can do it)

When shopping for a midwife make sure she is state certified, has a partner she works with (just in case she has 2 births at the same time), and most importantly is someone who makes you feel comfortable and secure. Your midwife should be someone you trust completely and love unconditionally.

There ARE midwives out there who are almost militant in their views- Homebirth is ALWAYS better and they will NOT refer to a hospital. Period. If you encounter one of these- run away as fast as you can.

No matter how much you may want a homebirth and for whatever reasons, the most important thing you can do for your child is to get him/her into this world safe and sound.

Just as you shouldn't have a hospital birth just because 'They' say it's safer, you shouldn't insist on homebirth if all indications point towards the hospital.

Weigh your options.

Listen to your head AND your heart.

And do me a favor- kiss the top of that baby's head for me.

Nothing is sweeter than a fresh new person.

The Unsung Benefits of Homesteading Or There's a Perfectly Good Reason For the Egg in My Pocket

Oh sure, we all know the perks of growing our own food, supplying our own energy and being as self-sufficient as we can be.

But what about the benefits of homesteading that AREN'T touted from the cover of the latest Mother Earth News?

Back when I lived in Wisconsin, Thanksgiving dinner was taken with my husband's family. They had a tradition that right after dinner, everyone gathered around the TV and they all watched Pay Per View Wrestlemania. As touching a scene as that was, with the little people all hunkered down in front for the best view, I just wasn't into it. And DARNIT! *I* had to leave early to go home and milk the goats. I know they all felt sorry for me- dragged away from the beer, cigarette smoke and surround-sound wrestling and forced to endure the clear cold country quiet and the company of companionable livestock. Somehow, I suffered through it.

Year after year.

When something breaks or otherwise needs mending around the place city folk get into the SUV and head for the Home Depot for the proper parts and the proper tools for the job. I have neither SUV nor the money for such extravagances as Parts and Tools.

Luckily, I DO have an endless supply of baling wire.

Homesteaders take multitasking to a level unheard of by most folks. We can feed the livestock, milk the goats, gather eggs, get breakfast into our families, have several loads of laundry washed and hung out to dry, the family washed and dressed and the whole crowd ready to face the day in less time than it takes for some of those Big Haired Women to do their 'do'. Of course, later in the day when your son needs a tissue and you reach into your jacket pocket and present him with an egg, it may be a sign that you need to slow down just a tad, but considering the workload still not too shabby.

There are a number of companies who provide home security. For a fee of course. We have a flock of guinea hens who work for chickenfeed, and when I asked the security fellas to supply me with some feathers for a mask my son and I were making, they just looked at me funny. Of course, the security guys don't roost up in the old oak and poop on my car, but I still prefer the guinea hens.

Children in the country are free to run wild and act like complete heathens without worrying about what the neighbors will think. Weather permitting, clothing is optional. My older son spent hours playing such games as "See how many long rusty nails I can pound into the picnic table" and "Breaking rocks with a hammer", and the young one likes to sit on top of the car and holler in some alien language (perhaps summoning the Mothership) when he's not digging holes or chasing the cats with the weed whacker (Just on the off chance that anyone in PETA is reading this, he doesn't know how to fire up the weed whacker yet so simmer down). My daughter played "Poke myself in the eye with a pointy stick", but just the one time. All three suffered from acute ADD- Acting Dang Demented, and I feel very sorry for kids who do all their running at the direction of the PeeWee Soccer Coach.

Men with homesteading wives do not have to enter a jewelry store or Victoria's Secret for holiday gift buying, but can head to the Tractor Supply or local hardware store- places they want to go to anyhow, and nothing screams Romance like a brand new shiny two-man saw.

And speaking of romance- forget the Dinner and a Movie nonsense. A man who does the evening feeding after working all day at a boring job to support his family, knows how to cook (and clean up after) a good simple meal, and enjoys sitting next to me with a cup of coffee in the porch swing to watch the baby goats gamboling in the yard beats the stuffing out of whatever soft yuppie male with a head full of 'hair product' that People magazine calls the Sexiest Man of the Year.

Call me strange, and a lot of people do.

That, my friends, is the biggest benefit of homesteading.

We are strange.

Not normal.

A little 'teched'.

There is nothing so freeing as being strange.

I don't have to wear the latest styles, or even know what they are.

I don't want a new car, or even a new truck. My old car gets me from point A to point B with little fanfare and little gas consumption, and even though BubbaTruck ('84 Silverado complete with gun rack) has moved across the road to Pa and Nana's place, I still have use of him when I need him.

I don't follow, nor do I care about the Desperate Housewives or Survivor. I'm too busy hauling feed, weeding the garden, hand washing laundry and stacking firewood to join a health club.

I don't have the time to worry about keeping up with the Jones's. I need to keep a step ahead of the weather, the grasshoppers, the weeds and the coyotes. (But hey, if the Jones's are good with a spade and a shotgun, they are welcome to lend a hand).

So strange I am, and I embrace my strangeness.

Because from what I've seen, being normal is just weird.

Mice- Scourge of the Homestead

When I was discussing options with my insurance agent, I asked if we could get MDI, and surprisingly, she had no idea what I was talking about. Apparently all the insurance companies cover are mundane things like tornadoes, fires, theft, and flood. Not a word about the most devastating disaster of all- Mouse Damage.

These tiny rodents are not only destructive, fast multiplying, and smelly; but they have unarguably the best Public Relations campaign in the history of Public Relations campaigns. From level-headed justice-minded Mickey Mouse, to pitiful lost Fivel and his hat that's too big for him in American Tale, to the singing mice in t-shirts helping Cinderella get ready for the ball, big screen mice are all small whiskered heroes. From the first time we hear "M is for Mouse" (unless you are Canadian where "M is for Moose") we have a warm fuzzy feeling regarding the little stinkers.

So the first time one makes a wrong turn and scampers across your feet, your likely reaction will be something on the order of "AAAIIIIEEEEE! (In midair, followed by a whole-body shudder upon hitting the ground), but then "AWWWWWW- it's so CUTE", and you will not only NOT be aware of the impending menace, you will consider yourself fortunate to have had such a close encounter with a little jewel of Nature.

Several days later, scanning the pantry shelf for a nice can of chicken soup, you will see them- and you will think to yourself "My, those mice are resourceful- leaving a trail of chewy mouse raisins to find their way back home, just like in Hansel and Gretl". It should only take a split second for your mind (the human mind being the marvel that it is) to discard the notion of mouse grocery stores selling mouse raisins for the express purpose of navigational convenience, and realize that what is actually all over your pantry shelves is MOUSE POOP.

This makes it an entirely different matter.

Right about then, still gagging from the idea of your food supply being used as a running rodent toilet, you will notice other subtle changes in the pantry. Everything that can be gotten into will have been gotten into. Cereal, pasta, bread, chips, anything not encased in metal or glass will have been tasted and tainted.

If the little darlings have been REALLY busy and REALLY hungry, you will no longer be able to find the chicken soup you originally came for since the label will have been peeled off and shredded. I've found tiny teeth marks on the lid of the peanut butter (in it's label-less jar), once had a tiny hole chewed though a full bottle of canola oil (with nary a drop of oil on the shelf- don't you know THOSE mice had really clean intestinal tracts), an entire batch of curing soap eaten through, and what made my son a lifelong Mouse Hater- a complete 10-pack of Yoo-Hoo in a Box's broken into and slurped down.

WOW you are thinking, this chick is a REALLY bad housekeeper!

A true enough statement, but not completely relevant to this topic.

This scope of damage can be done in an insanely short period of time. A single mouse can visit a feeding spot up to **200** times a night (it's true, I found it on the internet) and they have incredibly high metabolisms.

Well, that's YOUR problem you say- it's clearly your fault for living in a 100+ year old house that's about as airtight as a fishing net. MY house has things like windows that close properly and floors that actually meet the walls.

Mice are tiny. They are stealthy and they are apparently collapsible (like those tin cups you were issued in your Scout Mess Kit). Your average sized mouse has no problem fitting through the same square footage that the Lord's Prayer takes up on a grain of rice. If your home contains ANY spaces this size or larger from the Outside World to the Inside World, you will have mice.

Alrighty then, you say, confident smile on your face.

I'm a human.

Mice are rodents.

It would take the contents of 100 mouse heads just to equal the size of MY brain (give or take). I will put any food packaged in chew through containers in the fridge, the freezer or hermetically sealed mouse-proof bins, thereby solving the problem. If there's no food for them to get, they will go away.

If that were the case, this would be the end of the story, and according to my editor, I must submit a minimum of 1000 words, and we are just 300 words shy of that.

Mice will find food. Between the crumbs that fall on your floor, to the cat food in the cat dish (a cruel joke for the cat), there is still plenty of food to be had- especially if you are the caretakers of any fledgling people. If there are children in your house, you are the proud owners of one big ol' Super Mouse Buffet.

Once they have their food needs met, it's time for a little nap.

Or maybe a little procreation.

Or on a good day, both.

Mice will nest anywhere, but their preferred places seem to be inside a favorite pair of shoes in your closet, smack in the middle of a new roll of paper towels in the cabinet, or nestled snugly in a fluffy bed of the cloth that coats your electrical wires in between your walls.

Yes, having tiny brains even for their tiny heads, mice will not hesitate to partake in dangerous activities that will both kill them, and cause extreme stress for you and your pocketbook. Eating through cords both telephonic and electric, burrowing into the innards of a microwave oven, or doing a graceful swan dive into your drinking water cistern, the loss of one of their own is sad but not catastrophic, since mice are capable of truly epic reproduction. A female mouse is mature enough to have babies at the tender age of 8 weeks and can produce up to 40 babies per year. So if you start with one pregnant mouse in your kitchen, and given that 50% of her offspring will be females also, at the end of one year you will have…..ummm……a lot of mice.

Luckily, you will not have to fight the onslaught of this Lilliputian horde alone.

Mice attract snakes.

One year as we were battling the mice, we noticed their numbers waning and became smug. Looking for something in a rarely opened bottom cabinet, Ward found the real reason for our diminishing mouse population- a 3-foot long rat snake. The snake was highly offended by the invasion of his personal space and left through the tiny hole he'd come in through, never to be seen again.

Our mouse population blossomed.

The enclosed porch that is now my workroom at one point was home to my guinea pigs and cockatiels. When we converted it, we removed the cabinets against the wall and found an elaborate maze of trails that had been chewed into the particleboard floor.

Disgusted (Ward) and cursing (me), we swept up all the dusty refuse and bleached the whole place. Shortly thereafter I had a little shortness of breath. Looking up diseases on the internet (always dangerous), I found something called Hantavirus. Hantavirus is a disease that's transmitted by mice to humans, and is sometimes fatal. You get Hantavirus by inhaling dried mouse poop (like the dust in the air when you are SWEEPING IT INTO A DUSTPAN), and breathing problems are one of the symptoms.

Now panicked and more than a little miffed that my gravestone might read “Done in by mouse poop”, I called my family doctor, who looked up Hantavirus and told me that there was nothing to do pro-actively, and that I’d just have to wait out the ’14 days from time of contact’ for further symptoms to appear, since there’s no CURE per se, they just put you in the hospital when you are really sick, and treat the symptoms till you get better, or die.

I developed no other symptoms, but it sure didn’t add anything to my already low opinion of mice and I wanted them all dead.

But how to kill the little devils?

Aren’t cats supposed to be the ultimate mouse-eradication device?

Depends on the cat. A cat will hunt for one reason only.

Pleasure.

Cats do not hunt to find something to eat, and when you see a cat happily crunching on the head of something small and defenseless, it’s more of a victory dance than hunger relief.

I have one cat who was born to a life of luxury and lived completely indoors for his first few years who can take out 2 mice in a feed bag at once, and another who is wild as a March hare and I’ve never seen him kill anything, ever, in the 10 years he’s been living here.

I know of people who have put cats in their barns to kill mice and not fed them ‘so they’d hunt for food’. The cats either took off for a better place to live or died of starvation.

I have found that my toy poodles are excellent mousers. Smelling of foo foo spray, bows in their hair, toenails aglitter with polish, they are curly-headed demons when they think a mouse is around. Considering their size, I think it's therapeutic for them to pick on something that's actually smaller than they are.

One non-violent deterrent is stuffing any opening a mouse could fit through with steel wool, since they won't chew on it (so 'they' say). The problem with this is that you can never hope to find all those openings, and when you do, you should just FIX THEM.

Another natural deterrent is to soak cotton balls in peppermint oil and scatter them on your pantry shelves. The mice love this one since it's so tiresome just eating cereals and chips and so forth. If you leave little notepads and pens also, they will write you thank you notes for being thoughtful enough to supply them with dessert.

There are lots of anti-mouse devices out there, and most of them flat don't work. The phrase 'Don't try to build a better mousetrap' is right- the original is still the best. Let's look at some of the others.

Many people reach for the D-Con type poisons and they WILL kill mice.

Also small dogs and children who eat it and cats or chickens who eat mice who've eaten it. I've been in Emergency Animal care for too many years to recommend any way to use the stuff that's remotely safe.

Those 'sticky boards' they sell are just a laugh. Oh, sure you load the thing with peanut butter in the center and the mice WILL get stuck. For a minute. Then they are off, tummies full of peanut butter and just the loss of a little hair to pay for it. Pretty sweet.

Occasionally you will find a mouse in between eating the peanut butter and yanking himself off of the board, but what do you do THEN? Stomp on it? Gingerly put it in a plastic bag and wait for it to suffocate? Drown it? The whole thing is pretty unappealing.

And again, if you have pets, most likely THEY like peanut butter too. I have a vivid memory of my daughter's cat running through the house on his hind legs, sticky board attached to his entire tummy and front legs, clearly not amused and laying full blame for his embarrassment on yours truly.

There are things called Tin Cats that are little metal lock-ups with one-way doors. The mice go in, but can't come out. Once again, what the heck do you do with a metal box full of mice?

No, the clear choice is still the spring-loaded mousetrap. An inexpensive investment on your part, a quick kill for the mouse. The only two problems with the basic mousetrap are that sometimes you have to come dangerously close to touching a dead mouse to empty it (yes I use them over and over again, they're not THAT cheap), and if you are not possessed with lightning quick reflexes, there's the chance that you will get pinched setting the traps. I get pinched setting the traps.

Enter what is the only Better Mousetrap I've ever seen, the Victor Quickset, made by Victor- manufacturers of the original spring-loaded mousetraps. The Quickset looks like one of those big plastic clips you buy to hold your chips bag closed, so to set it, your fingers are out of the line of fire, and to empty it, your hand is on the opposite side of the trap from the carcass. And they are made of plastic, so there's less residual goo. Both the original Victor mousetraps and the newfangled Quicksets can be found at your local feed/hardware/building supply store, or online at www.victorpest.com

Armed with a case of Quicksets, snarling toy poodle at my side (OK, napping in my lap), wearing my horned Viking helmet (just because I like to wear it), I am ready to do battle with the Scourge of the Homestead- My Enemy Mouse.

In Defense of the Weedlot- Leaving Some Wilderness Areas on Your Homestead

Whether your homestead is one acre or one hundred acres, there's a terrific feeling of ownership and stewardship that goes along with knowing that YOUR land goes from 'here to there'. You know every tree, every bush, and every ripple in the landscape.

Paramount to being a good homesteader is economy- economy of money, of resources and most of all of your land. A lot of time and planning go into utilizing every inch to the best purpose. Especially with small acreages, it's tempting to 'domesticate' it all- from the vegetable garden to the woodlot to the pastures, the perfect homestead looks like one big AgExtention Calendar Cover, right?

Wrong.

Leaving patches of wild growth is good for the homestead and the homesteaders who dwell there.

First of all, it looks good. There is something very appealing about a patch of overgrowth pasture or untended woodland- like a living canvas; an ever-changing landscape of nodding blossoms, graceful grasses and twining viney things gently punctuates your homestead, softening an otherwise too-orderly-for-nature scenery and reminding us that we chose this life to escape from or as a protest to a sadly sterile suburbia.

Second of all, even a tiny wilderness provides an area just screaming to be explored by young Lewis and Clarks armed with plastic compasses, butterfly nets and warm oatmeal cookies nestled in their linty little pockets. If your place looks like a manicured subdivision yard, where is the benefit to your barefooted, country-raised youngens?

I mean, REALLY, if ya'll are going to tame the whole mess, you may as well have stayed tucked safely into 'Quail Ridge' (where they killed all the nasty pooping feather shedding quails and flattened the ridge to make way for row upon row of identical structures loosely referred to as homes).

Third of all, it's less work, and less work is good.

Oh sure, you could spend an entire weekend whaling the tar out of your fencerows, but if you just left them as a 'natural wildflower buffer' think of all the OTHER things you could be doing with that time.

You could build a greenhouse, learn to make cheese, teach your kids the difference between a moth and a butterfly by actually LOOKING at real wild moths and butterflies, hang a hammock and crawl into it with a good book, a glass of tea, maybe a cat, but absolutely no watch or clock in sight, heck- you could even study a foreign language (maybe Canadian).

Lastly of all, be aware of the fact that your land is not only yours.

This is not a commentary on the government or taxes or the government taxes, but a call to LOOK AROUND you at who you are displacing with every tree cut and every foot of garden tilled. Humans may be at the top of the food chain (something we like to say, even though there are plenty of life forms quicker, stronger and possessing of larger sharper teeth than we have) but if we push out all the other links there won't BE a food chain, just us and those things that are quicker, stronger and with larger sharper teeth.

Now I'm not a degree-holding scientist or a professional odds maker, but I do know where I'd put my money in a one-on-one contest of that nature.

Oh, I am aware that the large predators are endangered already by the domestification of the wilderness, and that if we insist on progressing with 'progress' the only links in the food chain will be us, cockroaches, mice and bacteria, (and the 'us' link will be extremely fragile at that point) but the image of a passel of Starbuck's toting, urban dwelling executives from say, Monsanto, rounding a corner and encountering a large cat is somehow perversely comforting.

We need to keep in mind that this land we claim to 'own' will be ours for but a nanosecond in time.

We currently 'own' several acres and have been here for 10 years. There's a big dead half-fallen pine in the back yard that has no bark on it, but at least 8 round holes that have been pecked or chewed around the top. Woodpeckers, squirrels and at least one family of hoot owls have made that tree their home off and on over the years.

There's a ½ acre spring fed pond down in the woods that has been home to beavers, fish, and lately a pair of blue herons who come silently sailing low across the front of the pines and veer gracefully behind them in and into the pond. The neighbor had a nice pond too, until he decided to shoot the beavers who were tending the dam.

On a much smaller, but no less important scale, for the first 4 years we lived here each spring brought a Luna moth to our kitchen window every night for a week or so. This was enchanting and amazing to me and I looked forward to when 'my' moth would return.

In researching theses creatures, I learned that they only live a short time after emerging from their cocoons- so short a time that in their moth stage they don't even possess mouth parts (a bad sign for a long life). This made me sad for the individual moths, but no less enchanted and awed by their visits.

Something had implanted my kitchen window as a stop in their genetic memories, and that was humbling. When they stopped coming, I was extremely saddened.

Obviously there had been a change somewhere in the environment. My kitchen window was no longer a convenient stop in their short lives and I hope fervently that the change was not something that I did in the name of making my farm 'better', since we've lost more than a big bug sitting on the window, we've lost some magic that was woven into the story of our farm.

I recall reading that the Perfect Lawn is a sterile environment. Those envied vistas of green, uniform in color and length, carefully maintained and diligently doused with Weed N Feed and insecticides, are as dead as the surface of the moon. Between the miles and miles of concrete we've laid and the poisons we've poured into the scraped parched soil to manipulate it into a false beauty, much of our earth is as appealing as a garishly painted mannequin.

After spending too much time in urban and suburban America, I return to the tiny speck of land that I call home, reeling from the stress that forced naturalness brings. My blood pressure drops with each truly natural sight- the wild daylilies under the chinaberry bush, wrens nesting outside the bedroom window in the overgrown untrimmed hedge, even the momentary glimpse of a coyote at the edge of the woods.

This is my home, but it's mine for a short time only. It is my pleasure and honor to use it gently for my needs, and preserve and protect it for the needs of all its other occupants.

Hair- Raising Homestead Haircuts

I'd like you to meet my son. He's six years old, cute as a bug and smart as a whip. Now where could he be? He was here just a minute ago...

No, wait! I see his grubby sneakers, his well-worn sweatpants with the collection of rocks and nails in the pockets, his unaccountably spotless Godzilla t-shirt. ACCKKK!

Where is his head? There is some sort of unruly tumbleweed kind of shrub atop his skinny little neck where his head should be!

In a panic only a mother can comprehend, I grab aholt of what appears to be some sort of alien invader engulfing my offspring's noggin. With a shudder of horror, I brush back the tangled menacing locks and find-

My son. Mildly surprised and blinking somewhat in the light, but I'd know those big browns anywhere. It's my son alright.

Looks like it's time for a haircut.

Cutting hair is not difficult. Anyone with a sharp pair of scissors and a modicum of patience can tame a head of hair with reasonable success.
Now, I'm not talking about anything fancy that will require curling irons, rollers or any type of styling goo.

For instance, here's the extent of my long hair cutting technique. Every so often, I will grab my hair, pull it around to the front, figure out by feel where it thins (generally about an inch from the ends), and whack it off at that point.

No, what I'm about to relate is strictly a very basic short hair cut suitable for men, boys, and females with shorter, cuter noses and better cheekbones than are possessed by yours truly.

The best place to cut hair is outside. You don't have to worry about the mess of hair everywhere, the lighting is good, and the vast outdoors takes the sharp edge off of the screams of any unwilling participants.

Grab your scissors and rustle up your head of hair to be cut.

Now, if this head belongs to your husband, you are in luck. All you have to do is tell him that his presence is required not to push/pull/fix/kill anything, but just to sit still in a chair for a few minutes in the sunshine while you massage his scalp and he'll be knocking down furniture and shoving small children and dogs out of the way to get to you. If you are also holding a brand new Sports Illustrated and his favorite beverage, the speed you will witness will take your breath away.

Just like shooting fish in a barrel.

If, on the other hand, the head is smaller and wilder, you will need another tactic altogether. As a parent, you are told to never lie to your children. Lying to children will teach them not to trust you. It will teach them to lie in return.

This is silly. Children are born liars. A child so tiny he can't even form words will emphatically shake his head in denial when asked if he's been in the cookie jar, crumbs cascading from his chubby chin onto his Buddha-like belly.

So instead of calling "Junior, time for your haircut", cheerily holler "Junior, time for ice cream for breakfast", or "Junior, it's raining monkeys outside", and when Junior rounds the corner at a swift trot, snag 'im with a stout rope and proceed to the front porch.

When my son was tiny, he had lovely locks of spiraling angel hair. He was over 2 when I finally resigned myself to the first haircut. I valiantly walked into Supercuts with the little guy, his curly locks were gone, and we returned home a grownup looking little boy and a mother in tears clutching a framed lock of hair. For some mysterious reason, his second trip to the barber went badly.

Extremely badly.

We left with about 1/3 of his head done at the request of the hairdresser.

Thus began my avocation of barber. The first year haircuts were accomplished with my husband's help. I'd cut hair frantically while he drew pictures with Alec sitting on the table. I never knew how adept my husband was at drawing some convincing renderings of motor vehicles in various colors and configurations.

Now Alec is a big boy and sits quietly, except for asking "Are you done yet?" after every snip, and shrieking "ITCHY ITCHY ITCHY!!!" after every fifth snip, and alternately peers at me appealingly or glares at me balefully through the falling hair.

Cutting Hair- the Actual Procedure

I will commence to share my exceedingly unscientific, completely untrained technique for clipping the average head of hair with unspectacular yet satisfactory results.

Step One- corral your victim (see above)

Step Two- wet the victim's head and towel dry. Comb out hair- the look we are going for here is something akin to a crowned crane whose just been goosed.

Step Three- facing your victim, gently pull up a hunk of hair, and measure off where you want to cut it using your fingers. The important part is to hold the hair vertically, not horizontally, as a horizontal cut will result in a look similar to Moe. On a bad day. Repeat all over the head, checking length once you are finished to make sure you didn't miss a spot.

Step Four- Once you have the entire head a uniform length, trim the back and around the ears. If you are dealing with an adult, clippers can be used at this point. For twitchy noise shy little guys you should be able to at least trim the back. You may need to forget about around the ears until they are less unpredictable.

Step Five- Brush off any stray hair, toss your victim into the shower for a good shampoo and rinse, thank your victim for not biting you and release back into the wild.

The Importance of Being Surveyed

Ten years ago I was overworked, underpaid, alone in the world and adrift without a home to call my own. That has all happily been remedied, but none of it has been without a lot of work, and even more luck.

I still work hard, but enjoy it much more. My financial reimbursement is more in keeping with the quality work I strive to deliver. Some people who like me, some who love me and some who are even content to live with me surround me. And I was fortunate to find this place I call home on a land contract purchase. It was a happy day when I signed papers to buy this place and an even happier day to receive the deed free and clear from our county tax office.

Interested, since I had never seen the legal description of my land, I playfully paced out my east lot line (the only one that's a pretty straight shot over pretty level land). I started at the north corner and counted out paces. I looked up when I reached what should've been the end.

Curious.

My house was up ahead of me by about 100 feet.

Confidently, I started at the other end of the east lot line and counted off paces. I looked up.

There was my house, teasing me from 100 feet away again.

This was potentially bad.

My mind has a wonderful way of being able to fly off in several directions simultaneously. I think there are medications for that...

My first thought was, "Very nice. I don't own my house."

My second thought was, "Who DOES own my house and will I have to buy it from them?"

My third thought was, "What's the cure for hyperventilation?"

Of course this all took place after 5pm so I got to stew on all the above till the next morning.

At 9:00am and 1 second the next day, I was on the phone with the tax office, anonymously, of course. (Like they couldn't see me on caller ID) I told them that 'this friend of mine' had a little problem with her legal description. Surprisingly, Tax Office Lady informed me that it was not uncommon for legal descriptions to be wrong
(Shouldn't they be called 'close guesses' then?), and that 'my friend' needed to talk to her neighbors to ascertain where THEY thought the lot lines were. If there was no argument as to their boundaries, all I had to do was have a new survey done according to the agreed upon area and file it with the tax office.

I have two neighbors- one on the south side and one on the north and west sides. The east side is a county road. South Side Neighbor said, "I just had my land surveyed when I bought the place and I KNOW that my lot lines are the corner posts of my fences. I am OK with you re-surveying using those posts as my corners".
One down.

West/North side neighbor is the bank president here in our little town and his family has been here forever and owns a lot of land. He said "I know MY lot lines are the fence posts and am OK with you re-surveying using those posts as my corners".

Bingo.

I called Tax Office Lady back (anonymously) and had two more questions for her to answer before I could breathe again. Since a new survey would cost over $500, and I did not have a spare $500 at my disposal, would it hurt anything to just ignore the situation for now? She told me the only way it could hurt anything is if the neighbors changed their minds regarding their lot lines. OK, I can ignore a situation. I have had years of practice learning to ignore things I can't change at the moment.

My second question was since 'my friend's' land was obviously larger than described, once I (I mean 'she') (sheesh) got around to surveying, would 'she' owe back taxes on the land 'she' didn't know she had? Tax Office Lady was quick to reply (lending more credence to the belief that this happens more often than you'd like to think) "no, but she will have to pay taxes on the newly surveyed piece once it's registered in the tax office".

Fair enough.

Years later, we were faced with tackling some large projects that we were neither young enough nor skilled enough to handle. These included new siding, a new roof, heating ductwork, and attending to electrical 'issues'. We had done everything we could on our own and paid as we went, but these were buggers. By the time we could save up to do the siding, the roof would've fallen in. By the time we could save up for the roof, the house would've burnt down from an electrical fire, and by the time we could save up for the electrical work; we would've frozen to death from lack of adequate heat. (Except for that few toasty minutes it would've taken for the house to burn down).

We bit the bullet and got ourselves a Home Improvement Loan.

Have I regretted getting the loan? Yes.

Have I fully appreciated the things we were able to do to our home with that money? Yes.

Are we repaying it as quickly as humanly possible? You betcha.

The POINT of admitting to getting this note is that we needed to get a survey in order to do it. (And also to let others know that sometimes we do things we don't want to do, and it's OK. There is a lot of talk about striking out to the country 'debt-free' and I admit that that's the way to go if you are diligent, plan well and are very very lucky. Do not consider yourself a Homestead Failure if you need a mortgage to get you to a place of your own. Just get the best deal you can, the best rate you can, and work like the Devil to pay it off as soon as possible. Paying an extra $100 each month on the principal can decrease the term of your loan by up to 50%)

Back to the POINT.

Our survey cost us about $800 and once registered with the county raised our taxes exactly zero dollars, since the land area was correct in the legal description, but the measurements were what were wrong.

We are now correct, recorded, and most importantly, our house is firmly planted on our land.

Now that we are looking at new land to move our house to, we are finding it exasperating that 10 times out of 10, the realtor will NOT KNOW WHERE THE LOT LINES ARE on a parcel. How the heck are you supposed to be expected to make a serious offer without that knowledge?

I guess if you are just looking for a hunk of land to plunk a McMansion down on, it doesn't matter how many trees there are, if the ridge or valley are part of the property or if that surface water is shared with another landowner.

It matters to me.

A lot.

Although I will not overlook a piece that states "no current survey available", if I got really serious about it, the seller and I would have to have a talk about getting one, and not at my expense.

A current, accurate survey is good insurance, both for the buyer and the seller. It is not a good feeling to stand at the end of your land and peer at your house floating independently of it.

Knowing EXACTLY what you are buying provides peace of mind, and in the world of homesteading, between learning new skills and the fickleness of crops and livestock; we need all the peace of mind we can get.

(Living in the) Sticks and the Single Girl

Carving out a homestead is a fantasy of many a young boy. Even now, when Saturday morning programming does not include anything like Davy Crockett or Grizzly Adams, there are still young boys whose dads and granddads go huntin', fishin', and card playin' up at the lake or river. Chances are, if those young boys have a sister or two, they are harboring similar fantasies as well.

Lucky is the gal whose dad takes her along on these treks to the woods and fields.

Luckier still is the gal whose MOM takes her fishin' and teaches her to bait her own hook.

I was a child of the late '50's and early '60's when men were Men, and women raised them. June Cleaver kept her house immaculate and always wore pearls and heels to BREAKFAST for Pete's sake. The moms from Happy Days, the Partridge Family and the Brady Bunch did the same. Heckfire, even Samantha on Bewitched who could do her housework by wiggling her powdered little nose didn't do much else all day long.

Oh sure there was Marlo Thomas, you know, That Girl. And Mary Tyler Moore. And Laverne and Shirley. THEY had jobs. But THEY were single. They were allowed. And it was always inferred that once they snagged a man, they'd be quitting that (whisper and spell it out) j-o-b, and having babies and simonizing the whole house along with the rest.

I was luckier than most as I was a Girl Scout back when scouting was still about camping and learning outdoorsy stuff. When **I** was a scout, we earned badges for fire making and knot tying, and our high school troop saved up for several years to go to the big Girl Scout camp in Wyoming for a week of primitive camping. Little girls loved riding the big hot stinky school bus to day camp in the summer where I was first a counselor, and later the camp director. We taught them how to lay a trail, build a fire, make stuff out of sticks and we ate s'mores and drank 'bug juice'.

By the time my daughter was a scout, badges were not stressed as much, and had been altered to be more 'relevant' to this new world (I was too depressed to even look to see what they changed them up to) and her high school troop saved up for a trip to Europe, where they stayed in hotels and shopped. The one time I volunteered to be camp counselor in this new age of scouting, the girls were delivered individually by moms in minivans and sat around complaining that it was hot, there was dirt, and they looked down their tiny perfect noses at me with scorn when I referred to the Kool-Aid as bug juice.

As a whole, Americans are a whole lot more urban than they used to be. This is no surprise to anyone, and for the most part this is looked at as a GOOD thing.

If you are a contemporary American couple looking for the simple life, it's hard. Your family and friends will suspect some sort of brain-damaging food poisoning. You will be looked at with amused and bemused affection and the barely-concealed suspicion that it's a passing phase that the male half of the couple is instigating to make up for some sort of failure in the corporate jungle. It is the female half of the couple's job to either talk him out of it, or go along with good humor till the phase is over.

And a lot of the time that is exactly what happens.

Sometimes a single male, perhaps after a divorce, will take off into the wilds to 'find himself'. This is accepted, even encouraged self-therapy. "Do the boy some good to get a little dirt under his nails. Build up a few muscles. Work out of the emotional doldrums" etc. etc. etc.

Here's where it gets weird.

Say you are a single FEMALE, perhaps after a divorce. If you announce to your family and friends that you are going to move out to the sticks and apply yourself to the pursuit of a simpler life, they will be coming after you brandishing anti-depressants and a straight jacket.

How will you live?

Won't you be lonely??

Who will take care of you???

Just smile sweetly and tell them it will do you good to get a little dirt under your nails, build up a few muscles and work out of the emotional doldrums.

There are a lot of resources on finding the right property. All those are unisex and depend not on gender for relevance. Sometimes you have to be a little more cautious depending on the realtor- some will think they can pull the wool over a 'little filly's' eyes on a place, but no more so than any other city slicker they see coming down the pike. The advantage of being female is that you are used to this attitude in most of life anyway and can smell a rat from a mile away.

With few exceptions, the manual labor of farm life is what will pose challenges. Although I've known women who could bench press the average tax accountant, most of us (collectively, not just females) are much much more weenified than in past generations. Renovating or building a homestead, working on fence, managing livestock, maintaining a kitchen garden, and general repairs will seem daunting, especially if you have to ALSO have employment off the farm to survive (and most of us do, don't feel badly if you need to also).

I have homesteaded with and without husbands and have to say that if your husband is not behind the idea 120%, it will be way harder than if you are by yourself. You will naturally be second-guessing and micro-evaluating everything you do all on your own; you will not need someone peering over your shoulder waiting to say 'I TOLD you that wouldn't work'. In such a case, some hard choices will have to be made, and those choices will depend on the personalities of those directly involved and must be made accordingly.

So.

You have found and moved onto your piece of rural paradise.

Now what?

You need tools. In addition to the tools you will find in the 'handy toolkit in a box' you can get at your local Home Depot, you will need a good sledgehammer, a good pry bar, a good hatchet and saw, a case of duct tape, an endless supply of baling wire, and a hot glue gun (for the delicate repairs).

If you possess a natural aversion to bugs, rats, mice or snakes, get over it.

If you are afraid of the dark, buy a really big flashlight and a lot of batteries.

If the complete quiet punctuated by the odd unidentifiable cry of a country night creeps you out, you have made a bad life decision.

To survive and thrive in the country as a single woman you need to always keep in mind the Three L's.

L number One- Laughter.

In the midst of your most frustrating day there is humor.

Your semi-feral Billy goat pushed over the fence and is now devouring your tomato plants after stromping all over the cucumber vines? Look at his face- calm, serene pride of accomplishment. Think of what YOUR face looks like. Funny.

Your car is stuck in what passes for the road because the rain you prayed for finally came? And you were on your way to have lunch with city friends in town and are now hiking back to the house wearing heels and stockings through the brambles and mud? Hilarious.

You are cornered across the room from the broom AND the door by a big ol' snake who happened to be napping under your kitchen sink? AND you have to go to the bathroom really bad? STOP IT, YER KILLIN' ME!!!

These are not at all humorous when you are in the middle of them, but stopping to try to find humor in a situation gives you the chance to catch your breath, calm down enough to come up with a plan, and make for some most excellent story-telling that will beat the tar out of your co-worker's harrowing tale of losing her car at the mall.

For example- one dark and stormy night I was sleeping in my house, minding my own business, when I was awakened by a tremendous BANG. Seems the furnace that had been installed that day was not leveled and when it kicked on, something inside caused a noisy malfunction of some sort. Speeding to the back of the house to turn off the furnace I couldn't help but notice out of the corner of my eye as I passed the kitchen door that the little copper tube that came up out of the floor where a fridge once sat and that carried water for the ice maker of said fridge had popped it's protective cap and was spewing water prettily into the air at an amazing rate of speed and velocity. After finding the 'water turn off key' (oh yeah- add that to your list of tools), I trudged out to the front of my property with a flashlight clenched in my teeth in the dark and the rain to turn off the main water valve. I returned to my cold, waterless house very un-amused.

And yet, in retrospect, it's hysterical. And part of the rich history I've made with this place.

L number Two- Leverage.

Females are usually smaller and weaker than males. It's a fact. I am at peace with the knowledge that no matter how many push ups

I do, or Power-Ades I slurp down, I will never be as strong as a male of comparable size. This is not necessarily a bad thing.

Sometimes it's an extreme advantage to think through a problem without resorting to or depending on brute force to do something. Because NO ONE is strong enough to literally tackle EVERYTHING.

Take working with livestock. There's this cow, see. It's eating happily but you need it to move to a different field. It likes THIS field.

You ask it to move. No response.

You yell at it. No response.

You yell at it while waving your arms. No response.

You yell at it while smacking it soundly on the rump. No response.

Placing a shoulder against the cow's shoulder, you try to push the cow.

The cow starts to giggle.

Because Mr. Universe is STILL not a match for your average, nay, your wimpiest cow.

You must apply leverage.

A well-placed thumb into the cow's ribcage is leverage.

So is a bucket of sweet feed.

Another personal anecdote- filling in at a Vet's office one day as receptionist, I watched the two male Vets and male owner of a mule trying to get the mule into the stocks for exam. They pulled. And pulled. And shouted. And cussed some.

Finally I went out there, wrapped the lead rope around the mule's butt so I was in effect pushing AND pulling the animal at the same time, and he quickly and quietly went into the stocks.

Find the leverage.

Embrace the leverage.

Use the leverage.

L number Three- Lashes.

Now this one is a last resort, but sometimes in order to get something done, playing the Damsel in Distress card is the way to go. You actually have a better chance at getting help, even free help, by being female than by being male.

If there's another country gal within easy distance to learn from, just ask. Most of us love to share our knowledge with others, and are always learning new things ourselves from OTHER women in an endless spiral of knowledge acquisition.

If all else fails, go on and ask a guy.

In general, guys will help other guys do things for the promise of a good card game and copious amounts of fermented beverage for the helpers after the job is done. It is still a learning experience for the guy who did the asking, but there's a price tag attached (gambling and beer).

In assisting a 'helpless female', your average guy needs no further payment. He's just "happy to be of assistance, ma'am. Holler if you need anything else". You have gained the knowledge that you need to do for yourself next time, and no hops or malts had to lose their lives for it.

Now, I'm not advocating donning petticoats and simpering (what IS simpering, anyway???), because if you have uprooted yourself and moved into the country you are already an independent, strong woman.

But the really good men out there whose mama's raised them right will be honored to help you and there's not a thing wrong with that. Plus, if you are right over their shoulder watching and handing them tools, or hip deep in muck along with them, you will also earn their respect.

And in the country, that's better than money.

I've never been laughed at or looked down on by my neighbors for trying to do for myself- in fact they've always been there to help and more importantly TEACH when I've needed it.

The biggest compliment I've ever gotten was from my 80-something neighbor.

I was helping him move some hay and at one point he squinted over the top of the bale and said 'you know, you're pretty good Help.'

Nothing anyone has ever said to me in almost 50 years has ever meant more.

Successful Transplants- Uprooting Your Urban Offspring

Every corner has been cut; every quarter has been squeezed. Diligently, doggedly, sometimes drearily, you and your spouse (if you have one) have toiled for what seems your entire lifetime to attain one shining spectacular end- the Family Homestead.

Giddily and even a little tearily, you call your beloved brood of loin-fruit to the tender circle of your parental embrace and announce “Kids- pack your stuff. We are moving to the country”.

There are cheers. There is palpable excitement. There is one child not jumping up and down and with a distinct cloud over her head. “Whatever is the matter, my dear?!” you exclaim in dismay.

The child in question does not move and seems for all the world to be carved in granite. Only her eyes turn their full attention to you, burning a hole in yours for a full minute before she utters three words slowly, clearly and unblinkingly.

“I’m not going”.

Now, this child may be 16, or she may be 6, but the one thing you absolutely positively must NOT do at this point is laugh. OK, two things- you must also not get angry.

Whatever the age of the offspring in question, their feelings about such a huge change in their life must be considered.

Now you could at this point dissolve into a puddle of shame, pull your child close and weep, “I’m sorry honey. What were we THINKING? Of course we will stay right here in the Mountainview Apartments, overlooking the spectacular Fast Food and Chain Store Range across the street! Now here’s twenty dollars- toddle off to the mall and make it all better”.

Or

You could take immediate offense and holler, "We have pert near kilt ourselves getting to this point and you are NOT an adult- you are our CHILD for pity's sake. You will do as we say and live where we go and when we say 'jump' you will ask 'how high?' DO we make ourselves abundantly CLEAR? If you don't like it- grow up, get a job, and move your sorry behind back to the city".

Now, the first reaction will make you miserable till your child grows up and moves out at which point you will realize that she has spent all your money at the mall and you no longer have the financial ability to move to the country, and the second reaction will make your child miserable till she moves out which in turn guarantees that YOUR life will be miserable, at least for the next (fill in the blank) years.

May I suggest as your third alternative, the Rules of Ate.

These are not really rules; more like steps.

And they have nothing to do with food.

And there are not eight of them.

But we are not talking about ME and my lack of cohesiveness. We are talking about a very serious problem with your child, and I'm just trying to help. You may thank me later. Or not.

Rule One- Validate.

The idea of leaving everything familiar behind and moving to a new place, even if it's only a few blocks away is stressful for the most hardened adult- think about the little person who's maybe never known another house or neighborhood in their life. If the child in question is old enough to go to school and have friends, the problem is insurmountable in their minds. Talk about and really listen to her fears and issues regarding the move and reassure her that you will do everything possible to make the transition a smooth one and promise (and mean it) that she will

NOT lose touch with her 'old' friends and will have a richer life for the making of new ones.

Rule Two- Recreate.

If you as a family have not spent much time without walls around you and ceilings above you, now is the time to take up camping. Work into it slowly. Start by taking Sunday drives out in the country with a picnic lunch. Move up to a day trip to somewhere outdoors encompassing several meals al fresco and finish your outdoors initiation with camp out- marshmallows, campfires, s'mores, the whole nine yards. While very few of us will actually BE camping on our properties, getting to be relaxed in the out of doors is a key ingredient to being content in a rural setting. If you can find homesteading workshops or 'reenactments' to attend and participate in, all the better.

Rule Three- Acclimate.

Spend time in your new neighborhood. Go to the grocery store, the feed store, and the playground. Visit the school and meet the teachers. If you are too far away to do this in person, take advantage of the Worldwide Web and travel via the 'net. Collect souvenirs from your new home in the form of newspapers, mom and pop restaurant menus, current school papers, park information, and community fliers about local events. Every little town has something that they are proud of- be it the yearly Marsh Marigold Festival or possession of the World's longest tapeworm. Find this and learn about it. Acclimation should also include finding comfort items, if only for reference. Where is the closest mall? The nearest Chuck E. Cheese? Knowing that these things are only X miles away will take the sting out of being thrust into unknown territories.

Rule Four- Meditate.

Brainstorm about what will be good about moving to the country. Think about what all of you will be doing in the way of chores once you are moved and mentally move through the days on the ‘stead even while living in the ‘hood. With your youngster’s friends, figure out a plan to keep them in touch, and start now- thanks to the internet, they can share via blogs, email and even websites. There’s always the telephone- buy a certain amount of minutes just for your child to call friends with every month. If you are not moving too far away, plan and carry out a slumber party at your new place, so your child’s friends have a concrete place in their thoughts to envision your child instead of just ‘to the country’ or ‘that stoopid farm’.

Rule Five- Instigate.

Make sure you save some of the ‘fun stuff’ for your children to do. If you are building a house, take their ideas seriously and if they are reasonably safe, do not break too many rules of physics, and are within your budget, let ‘em do it. Ditto for renovating an existing house. In the grand scheme of things, will there be a negative shift in the universe if your child’s room is painted purple? And if you are honest, aren’t the ideas of a tree house bed, a slide into the indoor tub or a skylight for stargazing before drifting off to sleep all pure genius? From planning, to budgeting, to shopping, to building and finishing, letting your child participate in this aspect of the homestead will cause her to set roots in it. Try to find out what outside aspect she finds appealing as well. Is she interested in gardening, animal husbandry, food preservation, record keeping, soap making, yak herding? Tell her to go for it and help her make it a successful venture- not so much financially as soul satisfyingly, but if it surprises you and brings in some cash, even better.

Rule Six- Create.

If you and your family have worked through steps One through Five, you are ready. Ready for the adventure of all of your collective lives. Ready for the tests, trials, successes and failures, and constant everyday learning that is referred to by those who flat don’t know any better as the Simple Life.

Welcome home.

Farm Dogs- See Spot Work

Most farms have at least one dog hanging around, and that dog may even do something to justify his free supper. If you are new to homesteading, or have somehow managed to remain 'dog-free' and are just now thinking 'hmmm, I think we need a dog', the following information may be useful.

Dogs have been the farmer's companions ever since the first dogs figured out that if they HELPED the farmer with the livestock instead of eating the livestock, the farmer was less likely to supplement his own diet with canine cutlets. Dogs have worn many hats on the farm, and still do. Since dogs come in many sizes and forms, they are a natural for specialization.

Your first inclination when thinking of a farm dog is probably Lassie.

Have a seat.

AKC Registered Rough Collie Lassie is a myth. So mythical in fact that the dog actor playing Lassie wasn't even female. Lassie was always played by male collies. (Good thing they have long hair, huh?)
Now, I have nothing against collies. I love collies. I've had collies and you will not find a sweeter, better natured dog around. But your general run of the mill purebred collie of today will have some issues. Collies are known for eye problems. Seems the breeders liked the look of the 'almond' shaped eye better than the nice round eye that can actually be seen out of and have bred collies with eyes that are literally suffocated for lack of air. A sleek narrow head was also found to be more attractive so they bred for that over a nice round skull. Now there's no room for a brain. Clearly a dog who cannot see properly and has a squished in brain is not going to be a very good 'working dog'. If you are itching for a good old fashioned 'farm collie' there really is such a thing. They don't look a lot like Lassie, but then, Timmy's yard did not look like a farmyard either. To find out more information

on Farm Collies, see (http://izebug.syr.edu/~gsbisco/fc2.htm) for people who are working with the old Scotch Collies- what the Lassie of the books probably really was.

Of course there's the OTHER collie- the Border Collie, and they are a completely different animal. Imagine Lassie on Speed.

If you have a very busy farm with a lot of stuff that needs tending, herding, sorting, worrying, then a Border Collie is perfect. Border Collies are arguably smarter than a lot of people and have a whole lot more stamina. Where Border Collies (and their families) get into trouble is when the dog does not have ENOUGH to do. Border Collies need to work and if you do not give them a job, they will make one up. Tearing up an entire household of linoleum is a short afternoon's work for a BC. Escaping from the yard just in case the NEIGHBOR has something to do takes about a split second if you have an average fence. If your fence is fashioned after the one at the maximum-security prison set into 3 feet of cement, it will take an entire second.

On a farm with plenty of work to do, a Border Collie can be an invaluable companion- sharp, quick; always ready for any adventure you may have to go on no matter the weather- just the chance to be DOING something with you will be met with an exuberance that's rarely found for something short of winning the lottery. The big one.
For more information on Border Collies, see (http://www.americanbordercollie.org/)

Farms harbor vermin. It's a fact. You can deny it, you can ignore it, but they are still there- mice and rats will be wherever there is a food source and that means your farm. Terriers have been bred to dig out vermin- the word 'terrier' comes from the Latin word 'terra' or earth, so they are literally dogs bred to 'go to earth'. The most commonly known terrier right now is the Jack Russell Terrier; thanks to the TV show 'Frasier' and Eddie their dog. Today's terrier WILL kill mice and rats. Unfortunately, like the Collies, the terriers of today are usually so far away from being working dogs, that they are indiscriminate in their prey and will seriously deplete your flock of chickens as quickly as your mice.

Back in high school I worked on a poultry farm where the house pet dog was a Cairn Terrier. Like Toto in the Wizard of Oz. Now, if you recall, Toto was a farm dog and there were chickens blowing by during the tornado that he had not killed. The terrier on the poultry farm, however, was kept firmly chained when outside because if loose, he had been timed at killing a chicken EVERY 30 SECONDS till caught. My own flock of hens was recently diminished by the Jack Russell Terrier down the street, and the neighbor gave up on chickens because her rat terrier made short work of them.

For a large terrier, an Airedale is a good choice. When used as working farm dogs they are more for guarding and pulling carts, but individuals can be gifted as herders and hunting dogs as well. They are usually good babysitters and are strikingly handsome.

Be very careful with small terriers. I currently have a crossbred terrier who is wonderful at not killing chickens. She does not kill mice either. She will absolutely tear up a rogue cookie however. In fact my best mouser, up to and including any cats I've had is my 4-pound toy poodle. Go figure.

If a terrier is appealing to you, do your homework and find some out of 'farm working stock'. Here would be a good place to start (http://www.terrier.com/breed/working.php3) for Jack Russells and (http://airedale-nawata.tripod.com/nawata/index.html) for Airedales.

There are a lot of other 'specialty' dogs who fit in on the farm- previously we discussed the Livestock Guardian Dogs in an article devoted just to them.

The hunting dogs- pointers, hounds, spaniels and retrievers are all good choices for farms where hunting is part of the routine.

Every once in a while you will find by accident a dog who is completely suited for a job on your farm- my four pound poodle is a good example.

And of course, there's nothing quite like a good mutt. Employing a mixed breed dog can be a very good thing. They are usually much more inexpensive as far as initial outlay for purchase. There are people who believe that the mixed breeds possess 'hybrid vigor' making them less prone to health problems. This is not true. I've seen just as many mixes with hip dysplasia and skin conditions as purebreds. The best reason for getting a mutt is that they usually really need the home, and although I'm not one for anthropomorphism, I truly think 'rescue dogs' tend to try a little harder to be Good Dogs than their counterparts who were born into good situations.

Even with the best of intentions, common sense must play a factor in choosing your mixed breed. Collie/Shepherd/Retriever crosses are a good bet. Chow/Pit/Rott crosses may not be. Individual dogs will be as varied in temperament as in looks, so blanket assumptions should just be guidelines, not set in stone rules.

Just like everything else on the farm, your dog will need regular maintenance and upkeep. A good quality dry dog food should be given twice daily- especially with the larger breeds, multiple small meals lessen the possibility of gastric torsion (usually fatal, always expensive), and in all breeds, food is just assimilated better if not given in one big meal. Regular worming and vaccination schedules should be adhered to according to your local laws and climate. External parasites need to be kept to a minimum. Expect yearly upkeep expenses on your dog (not counting food and squeaky toys) to be several hundred dollars.

A good dog is as valuable an asset as anything else on your homestead, with the added benefit of also being your friend.

Lilac Moon- Homesteading in Northern Minnesota

A good while back I read a book whose author and even title evade me now, but one segment of the narrative has stuck with me. It was a telling of how a particular area had been 'settled'. Prospective farmers would be issued a deed to a piece of land, they would timber it, plow it, plant it, harvest it, and repeat. Till it was used up. Then they would move on to the next piece. It was a badge of honor to say 'I've wore out (X number) of farms.' The signature of the hand of Man on the land is generally an ugly one.

But there is a place.

A place where the goal has not been domination, but co-existence with the land- and both the land and its residents of all species have flourished.

Come with me to Lilac Moon in northern Minnesota.
Now normally, when you think of a homestead that is powered by the sun, regulated by thermal mass and as lush a piece of Eden as can be imagined by the mortal mind, the first hundred or so geographical choices do NOT include Northern Minnesota.
And yet, here it is.

Exiting the Interstate highway for the four lane through mid sized towns, thence to the two lane that wanders through smaller hamlets and onto the gravel road into the bosom of the state forestlands, it's very easy to drive right past the unassuming gate marked with the tiny lovely sign "Lilac Moon".

Winding down the soft drive lined with generations of leaves and pine needles is the closest a motor vehicle will ever come to 'padding on little cat feet'. At the end of the drive, once the engine is turned off, the silence is deafening.

Here in the middle of this forest is a clearing that looks not so much 'cleared', as 'gently borrowed'. A vegetable garden naturally fenced and gated produces wildly and with abandon, punctuated with riots of flowers. An elderly apple tree shelters a solar shower, sink and soap. Next to the garden is a well-placed hammock with a view of both the garden and the forest, which lies just beyond a wide edging of native flowers. A fire pit ringed with stones awaits cooking duty, followed by being the focus of good company and perhaps good music.

The caretakers and human residents (I balk at the use of the word 'owners') of Lilac Moon are Bruce and Cheryl, who have been here since the early '80's. It's apparent in the many touches and forms here that this place has not so much been 'built', as has evolved.
This in itself is genius, and worthy of extreme merit.

Let me momentarily digress.

Most of us, when planning our homesteads, especially our residences, are wont to think- I need X, XXX square feet of living space, because SOMETIMES we have people over for shindigs, and SOMETIMES I have to do canning, and SOMETIMES we have overnight guests. Here's the genius part. B and C have several DIFFERENT structures, all within sight of each other, all built completely differently and all with a different purpose. Therefore, the only living space that they need to employ at any given moment is what they are actually using at the time.

Genius.

Back to Lilac Moon.

Let's start with the main house. Where your average residence perches atop the ground like a boil on a giant bum, this home is part of the land itself. Banks of windows facing the sun peek out from under a roof of earth shaded by lushly meandering squash vines. The exposed stucco surface is shielded by mounds of blooming plants, beckoning towards the interior. Remember how cozy that blanket tent under the kitchen table was when we were little? Same feeling.

One of the main arguments against earth-sheltered homes is the assumption that there must be a cave like feel to them. With the warm wooden beams and paneling- all harvested from this very piece of land forming the ceiling and walls, and the sun streaming in the windows, the word ‘claustrophobic’ does not even enter your mind.

This lovely little gem of a residence consists of a small but well planned and stocked kitchen with both gas and wood stoves and a sink with a hand pump to bring water from the well directly underneath,

Cozy living room, library/office area and a bedroom, all surrounding the substantial rock sauna/woodstove.

Tucked away to one side is the battery storage bank that connects to the solar panels on the roof.

Down a peaceful birch-lined path is the outhouse, a tiny little room that is brighter and cleaner than most peoples’ indoor bathrooms (including my own). Waste treatment here is by use of a sawdust toilet and then to the compost pile, and the only thing you smell on entering the outhouse is the pleasant scent of wood shavings. It’s not buggy. It’s not odiferous, it’s not primitive. It’s overwhelmingly sensible- much more so than a system that takes fresh drinking water to flush bodily wastes back into the environment. And did I mention how cute it is?

Behind the house proper is the garage/workshop/office- Bruce’s domain. This is a reasonably ‘mainstream’ structure, the office part being the newest section with a wall of windows overlooking a wooded ravine. A small woodstove keeps it toasty in the wintertime. (Note to forum members- when Bruce is being Lodestar on the forum, this is where he’s sitting- windows to the left, wall of books behind, woodstove and futon for the cats ahead).

There are several woodpiles on the property, and all are stacked, sorted, sized, and split according to need and use in a display of organization that I can only hope to accomplish in my wildest dreams.

Back towards the garden and fire pit is the summer house- a screened room that accommodates guests in warm weather, facilitates outdoor cooking, and is a welcome retreat from mosquitoes when they are in season.

Cheryl's studio is a ½ mile stroll through the woods and around the wetlands. A straw bale structure, it staunchly pooh poohs any notion that straw bale must only be done in warm, dry climates- for northern Minnesota is neither. The secret, we are told, is in the overhang- there MUST be enough overhang so that the body of the building does not get rained/snowed on. The thickness of the walls gives a muffled feel to the interior, calming and relaxing, but uplifting and positive thanks to the light stucco finish and large windows. A second vegetable garden, another outhouse and the earth-sheltered greenhouse are also nearby.

The permeating aura of the entire homestead is one of complimentary alliances- forest and garden, structure and nature, self-sufficiency and inter-dependence. And at the heart of the homestead are the homesteaders themselves.

Bruce and Cheryl are one of those truly great timeless couples that you must refer to together like Fred and Wilma, Hansel and Gretel, Ben and Jerry. Singly they are phenomenal- Bruce is explosive power and determination, constant motion and mental wheels always turning. Cheryl is every bit as powerful in a quiet, calming, gentle and deliberate way.

Together they are indomitable.
Together they have taken a beautiful parcel of forest and gently molded it into more than a homestead.
Once you pass through the gate at Lilac Moon, beyond the silence, beyond the beauty, beyond the very real workings of a homestead, is a quiet certainty that this is a home.

Earth Stewardship 101- Part One

I grew up a city girl in Wisconsin on a city lot of 50 by 100 feet. In the backyard we had 2 rose bushes that pre-dated our residence and came up year after year blooming with abandon. One summer I installed a rock garden back under the big trees where I transplanted (with permission) wild flowers from the Girl Scout camp. Most of them endured, and some even thrived. One year my mom planted a solitary zucchini plant and we ate zucchini in EVERYTHING for months. Those 87 words completely encompass my early life experiences in earth stewardship.

My entire focus as an adult has been one thing- escape to the country. After a brief stint at apartment living, and then seven years living in my grandparents' house that they sold us, we did it- bought 3 acres outside of town.

Within several years we had a large garden, dairy goats and three horses. We had a huge yard, a tiny pasture that we guarded fiercely against over grazing and the rest was dry lot- three horses and about a dozen goats turn an acre of grass into an acre of dust pretty quick. Luckily hay was readily available and cheap- $2.50 per bale delivered for alfalfa.

After moving to Texas and spending several years in a trailer park, I was able to buy 3 acres and an old house via land contract. Over two acres is wooded and we LIKE the woods, so our garden is postage stamp sized, we've no place for fruit trees and once again our dairy goats and horse are on dry lot, but this time there is NO pasture, even a tiny one. And thanks to two years of drought, hay is a precious and elusive commodity- WHEN I can find it; it's $9.00 per bale and usually sticker ridden and/or some musty. While other people dream of bigger homes, newer cars, expensive vacations to exotic places, our Rural Quest has been one thing- a bigger piece of land, where we can supply our own food, our own water, and our own pasture and hay. Although A LOT of land would be lovely, all we need is 'enough'.

We looked at lots of land- every weekend was devoted to driving through the surrounding countryside looking for something not too far from where we are now since we have roots in this little town and don't want to leave it. Although we walked over acres and acres of places, we saw nothing we wanted to leave our own place for- even though it's too small for what we currently have and want to do in the future, it's a gem of a place- century oaks, towering pines, and a ½ acre spring fed pond that's never been murky and is only down about a foot even though our rainfall is down almost three feet in the last two years.

One day I drove past a newly listed place on a whim- from the description in the ad I didn't even have medium hopes of this fitting our needs. And yet…when I drove up to the gate I just knew. I called the realtor before calling my husband. The next day we walked all over it and signed the initial contract on the hood of the realtor's truck. Banks, appraisers, surveyors, title companies and several months later, we signed the final papers and were handed the key to the gate.

You know how when you buy something new, once it's really yours you start noticing little flaws you didn't notice at first? That hasn't happened here. Every time we go out there we love it more. But love won't accomplish what we need to do with this place- protect the precious natural resources that we have while coaxing every inch to be all it can be. At twelve acres it is certainly enough, as long as we use it and care for it wisely.

And that's where the panic sets in. Neither one of us has ever HAD a place that could provide for us almost completely. And how to accomplish our goal of a sustainable, flourishing farm has as many answers as folks with an opinion to offer. So we are calling in the 'experts', gathering all the information, deciding what makes the most sense to us, and will do what seems the best for our speck of earth.

Our first expert was Julie, District Conservationist for the Natural Resources Conservation Service. Julie met us out at the property one afternoon and walked over it with us. She spent almost two hours going from one end of the land to the other. And she does this for FREE, through the courtesy of our tax dollars. Something tangibly useful. How cool is THAT?

Seeing the spring fed branch that meanders across the place, she gazed at it a moment- running clear when most creeks much larger are dusty channels and even some huge lakes have disappeared in the drought, and quietly commented- “that right there is a Gift”. When I expressed a desire to have a pond dug out in a bend of the branch, she said that altering a named branch in any way is not allowed without a mass of permits, a barrowful of cash and the invitation of the ACE into your immediate family. She offered ideas to pump water up out of the branch with the help of a ram pump for the livestock OR we could just let our resident beavers keep building the dam they’ve been working on and we’ll have our pond. Go beavers.

She told us to wait to do water and soil samples till February, since the drought is affecting the results of both types of tests- everything is so darn dry the readings are all skewed. Hopefully we’ll be recovered some by then in the rainfall department.

Her recommendation is to plant one of a variety of hybrid Bermuda grasses in both the pasture and the hayfield this February and in the fall sow a winter grain like rye in the pasture to provide graze through spring and clover in the hayfield as a green manure.

When I asked about native plants to introduce on the creek banks to hold soil against erosion, she said just don’t cut the trees on the bank and the roots will keep the soil. Unfortunately, a lot of our trees’ roots are becoming exposed and the trees are leaning across the creek trying their best to hang onto that dirt. It seems to me that there are smaller plants that could help the trees.

A totally unexpected piece of information that Julie provided to me regarded the electric poles (small single wooden ones, not the big multi-wired metal monsters) that march through our wetland area and across part of the front of the property. I need to call the electric company ASAP because they come out in helicopters and drop defoliation chemicals to keep the area under the poles clear. Considering the spring activity in the wetland and the proximity of the creek to the front of the property I see this as BAD. She told me her husband works for the electric company and if I call them and promise to keep the area under the wires mowed; they will come out and flag the boundaries of our place, keeping the helicopters away.

I like Julie. She gave me some good ideas and I expanded her knowledge of dairy goats, something she's wanted to learn about. Several weeks after her visit, we received a nice report in the mail from her including a topographic map, a soils map and corresponding soil chart, and two aerial maps- one from two years ago and one from ten years ago. There are also flyers about the different varieties of Bermuda grass, one on prescribed grazing, one on pest management using planted clover to choke out weeds since I expressed our desire to do as little with poisons as possible, two on pasture and hay land planting (guides for using the different Bermudas), and a flyer on purchase and installation of ram pumps (both hydro powered and solar powered) to move water into water tanks keeping livestock out of the creek.

Now, most all the farms around here that want high yields of fine quality hay will plant, fertilize and cut Bermuda grass. The small niggling unease I feel about Bermuda grass is that it's not native and horrendously invasive.

My next call will be to the Texas Parks and Wildlife Dept. biologist. Like my new friend Julie, the TPWD biologist will come out free of charge. They have programs to restore NATIVE grasses and forbs for pasture and hay management that include the lending of special 'no till' planters to minimize erosion, and I'm thinking that since I'm mostly feeding goats (who are browsers, not grazers) that having a mixture of things, even in the hay, would be a good thing. I believe that they will also be able to give me a better idea of 'edge' type native plants to keep erosion at bay on my creek banks, and hopefully some guidance for what to plant/nurture/harvest in our spring rich wetlands area.

As purty as a field of bright green Bermuda hay is waving in the breeze, I'll be willing to bet that a meadow of wild grasses and flowers would not only be purtier, but actually easier to maintain without a lot of human and chemical input. There's an appeal to restoring an area to natural health and I'm excited at the prospect of both helping wildlife and being able to sustain us simultaneously.

Of course I don't know for a fact it'll work that way, but we're fixin' to find out.

Earth Stewardship 101- Part 2

Wild turkeys are fickle things.

The Texas Parks and Wildlife biologist who was going to do our land assessment had to reschedule our rescheduled (due to inclement weather) appointment because the turkeys that were going to be transplanted arrived early, causing all the TPW biologists to flock to West Texas for the event. (Apparently this is done in the winter, so the turkeys are dormant and can't peck you while you stuff them into the ground)

We finally got to meet Heidi on a sunshiny afternoon, and while Julie had been looking at our place through Agricultural Traditional Farming eyes (and there's nothing wrong with that), Heidi was seeing it as Wildlife Habitat that would also support a small family farm. I found Heidi by doing an Internet search on establishing native pasture, which steered me to the Texas Upland Game bird Restoration Program. My completely uneducated guess is that every state has Parks and Wildlife biologists who will be eager to talk to you regarding making your homestead a friendly place for wild things to call home.

Starting from the lowest point on our land, we hopped from marsh mound to marsh mound as she pointed out different types of ferns and water plants. Heidi explained that as odd as it sounded, the parks department recommended doing controlled burns on wetlands (?) because all the mounds that made for such convenient hopping were actually too old to be very appealing as food for ducks and geese, and that burning would encourage new growth and bring in the waterfowl.

Surveying the eroding banks of our creek beds, she made notations of plants that would work well holding that precious soil in place- most notably viney things that set down roots every few feet like trumpet vines and passionflowers. Wow. How pretty would THAT be? Peering up at the tall trees lining the creek and spring branch, she said that there were several prime spots for Wood Duck nest boxes and asked if I'd be interested in having her send us a few. WOULD I? WOOD I? You betcha, boy howdy! I've only caught brief glimpses of these most beautiful of ducks in the wild, plus the nature documentary showing baby ducks leaping from their nest dozens of feet above the ground (and in almost agonizing slow motion), having the time and air space to execute several acrobatic feats and then land on the leaves and moss once, twice, sometimes bouncing three times before their little webbed tootsies stay in contact with the earth for good and they march with serious intent to the water.

In our future orchard and pond area Heidi picked up one of the spikeyballs that do an excellent job of protecting the ground from bare feet (along with the grass stickers) and asked Alec if he knew what it was. Now Alec's mother has TOLD him what those are. But there is a vast, enormous, totally un-spannable difference between your MOM telling you something, and Heidi the uniformed, blond biologist who drives the new pickup with the seal of Texas on it telling you something. Alec can now tell you that the spikeyball is the seed of a Sweet Gum tree, can point out a Sweet Gum seedling, and show you the adult parent Sweet Gum tree. Whatever.

Moving on to our teensy beginning of a vegetable garden, she noted that the deer have already discovered our two berry bushes (ok, berry twigs) and recommended fencing the garden ASAP. At this point we hadn't even crossed over the creek to the hay meadow and she asked "Are you SURE this is only 12 acres?" I assured her that according to the spanking new survey, it IS 12.02 acres and that in fact that since 1 of those 12.02 acres includes the county road, two wooden bridges and between 2 and 4 feet on the other side of the road, and at least another acre encompasses the creek, spring branch and accompanying meandering wooded banks, it's more like 10 acres, 2 of THOSE acres wetland (or as we refer to it here in East Texas- 'bottoms').

Hiking to the top of the hill, Heidi pointed out a stand of brambles and wild blackberries, milkweed (showing Alec the silky seeds in the pods and explaining that milkweed is the only food eaten by Monarch butterfly caterpillars), and happily amazed that there was no introduced Bermuda grass. If there had been, the parks department has a program that will give landowners, for free, the secret powerful poison to kill the highly invasive Bermuda grass in readiness to re-establish the natives. I told Heidi that we are only the third recorded owners of this place and that no one has ever lived on it, ever.

Catching our breath under a giant Sweet Gum tree at the top of the hill (home of Alec's future tree house), our neighbors' 25 acre woods behind us, across the tiny county road to over 400 acres of wild bottoms held by out of state owners and a family trust in front of us, hearing nothing but the wind and the birds despite being only 3 miles out of town and a 4 lane highway, Heidi looked at me and said "I go out on a lot of these assessments, and I can tell you this is by far the nicest small acreage I've been on in this area." Little did she realize how dangerously close she was to being hugged by an old hippie chick at that moment.

The recommendation for the hay meadow was to do a controlled burn (again with the burning…) and then sow it with native grasses and wildflowers.

I was promised a report in the mail suitable for submission directly to the county appraisal district to apply for our 'Wildlife Habitat Management' tax credit. To keep this in effect, we need to actively fulfill three of TPW's list of recommendations per year and submit them with photos and receipts (if applicable) to the appraisal district. So this year if we put up the wood duck nest boxes, do the burn/native grass planting in the hay meadow, and use Ward's night scope that he got for Christmas to do a wildlife census, that's our three. If we do the wetland burn, establish native flowers to attract butterflies along the roadsides and start planting viney things on the creek banks next year that's another three. Adding onto or doing something to maintain or improve things we've already done count as well. So (since we have such a long stretch of creek banks) we'll specify where, what, and how much is planted each year.

The official report that Heidi sent me states our Objective as- "to improve and enhance the habitat for white-tailed deer, songbirds, waterfowl and other game and non-game wildlife for conservation and recreation purposes in conjunction with running a small family farm. Likewise, managing and maintaining healthy, diverse, and sustaining populations of wildlife will create personal satisfaction in providing quality stewardship of the property." I like it.

Of course a big part of the 'small family farm' equation means providing our livestock with food as close to year round as we can. My feeling was that since goats are not really grazers, but browsers, instituting rotational grazing of a meadow of mixed grasses, forbs and legumes would actually be better for them than a diet of straight fertilized Bermuda, but I wanted to be sure, and also be comfortable tossing my little Arabian mare into that mix. I called my goat Vet, who's known me for over a dozen years and likes me anyway.

Dr. Wilson was emphatic both in his assurance that my stock would not only do fine, but thrive on that type of management, and that considering the relatively small acreage involved and the fact that it is on a hill, it may be difficult to interest anyone to come cut and bale Bermuda grass for us, not to mention the necessity of fertilizing the darn stuff every year, native is the way to go. He was also quick to point out that the whole 'wildlife habitat restoration/non-chemical natural organic pasturing' concept is just more 'me' in every way. I think he meant that in a good way, but sometimes it's best not to demand too much elaboration.

Heidi had given me names of several professional firebugs who do controlled burns for a living. She recommended calling the fire dept. and having them on hand 'just in case'. I decided to see if I could do away with the middleman and called our volunteer fire dept and asked if they would be interested in burning off the meadow as a training exercise. The excitement at the prospect was evident over the phone line. They will be HAPPY to come set our field ablaze and only ask a donation in return. As soon as we get the correct timing and combination of rain followed by fair and calm weather, we'll be witnessing (and Alec will be cheering) the conflagration of sticker burs, stinging nettles and goat weed (which I've learned is actually one of the only things that goats WON'T eat). Once the ground cools off we'll be ready for

Planting. Native American Seed Co. (http://www.seedsource.com/catalog/index.asp) was a seed source highly recommended by Heidi. Jayson, my new friend at Native American Seed Co., spent a goodly amount of time counseling me on the phone. Although his company has several lovely mixes of native grasses and wildflowers, when I told him the acreage we were working with and what we wanted to accomplish with it, he figured up a custom mix that would be both nutritious and successional just about year round. (Insert chart) All these plants are either perennial or self/free seeding, giving us a permanent pasture that will need no fertilizing and be really pretty to boot. Being accustomed to not running into too many 'goat people' in the general populace, I was surprised (and impressed) when I mentioned reading that Maximillian sunflowers are a good source of protein, and Jayson asked me if we had dairy goats or meat goats. Apparently, this sunflower imparts kind of a musty taste to the milk, so although it's very good for them, we need just a smidge or the milk will be…unpalatable.

Of course, such customer care comes at a cost. This sack of custom mixed seeds has a price tag that stopped my heart for just a moment, but then I got out the calculator and figured out that even if it feeds the critters for only 6 months out of the year, we'll have broken even in the first year.

Nowhere in any plan do the words 'till' or 'plow under' show up, and that's good for several reasons. First of all, we don't have a tractor. But more importantly, remember this parcel is a hill, and tilling it under, even carefully, would wash some of the topsoil downhill and into the creek. And if it were to rain anywhere between the 'tilling' part and the 'seeds sending down really deep roots' part, all our plant embryos will end up in a sad pile at the bottom of the hill. No, our plan calls for the exciting, high tech technique of one of us walking along our scorched land, hand broadcasting seeds, while another follows with one of those big rolly things to tamp them just barely underground.

Having both Julie and Heidi do evaluations of our land was a worthwhile and eye-opening experience. Both are wonderfully professional, friendly and helpful. The information and recommendations made, and reports compiled, would have been an excellent investment and it's just frosting on the cake that their services come free for the asking. I strongly suggest that every landowner, whether just starting out or already established, avail themselves to their own county or state's biologists. Having your land looked at through different eyes can open up possibilities you may not have considered that will simultaneously enhance your land and enrich your life.

So we have an initial plan. Not an orderly, groomed, intensive, every square inch toeing the line kind of plan. More like a restoring the land to what it grows willingly and well and rejoicing in the wild diversity of it kind of plan.

Dr. Wilson is right. That IS 'more me'.

Living Upscale Downhome

Ya know what I hate?

I hate leaving the farm.

For almost any reason.

Leaving the farm means that I've gotta get in my CAR, take it on the ROAD, and go somewhere there will most likely be PEOPLE.

I hate that.

Because people as a general group and I have not a whole lot in common nowadays.

There are times that I am thrust into a social situation where what I do and how I do it down on the farm are just not considered normal. Now on most given days I consider that an excellent gauge of whether I'm on the right track or not- the farther from 'socially normal' I am, the closer to my ideal.

But there are those few times, no more than several a year luckily, that I must for whatever reason, pick out a Sunday Go To Meetin' dress (no pantyhose, I draw an indelible line there) that covers my tattoos, find a pair of shoes that has NOT seen the inside of a chicken house, paint on the L'Oreal Soft Fern eye shadow and the Naked Ambition lipstick (yep, got it just for the name), and break out the Dressy Velvet hair scrunchie. Once all gussified and at whatever social event merited such foolishness, I then have to be SOCIAL. With PEOPLE.

Here's where the problem starts. Because apparently, 'normal' people talk about things like going to the gym to workout, the merits of different imported coffees and the latest sale at the mall. There are two main themes to the conversations- acquisition and self-improvement.

Well, that's not quite fair. Sometimes they also talk about their children's' acquisitions and carefully planned and supervised free time activities.

For a while, this bumpkin was at a loss at these types of social functions, having nothing considered of value to say and all, but now I actually look forward to them. I'll gracefully slide on into the midst of the group and wait for someone to politely ask me what WE'VE been up to?

"Oh Sugar (sweet smile) we've been so frightfully busy what with the Alternative Lifestyle Implementation since as you may know we've located our domestic headquarters in the financially advantageous Rural Renewal area.

We recently traded up on that minivan and got a fully loaded recycled multi-purpose vehicle with cargo room to spare, custom seat covers and the convertible RV option.

The house is a wonder, and there's no denying that. It has a full flow thru ventilation system, a rooftop-based whole house-humidifying feature, and more than ample storage in the open-air basement.

Naturally, security is always an issue, and we have installed the best in home guardians. For a minimal outlay in expense and upkeep, our personal crime deterrent will patrol the entire fence line a minimum of once per hour, sound an audible alarm if it senses any movement within it's range, and as an added bonus, it even keeps track of the children.

And it was such a HASSLE driving all the way to the gym, that we now have our own (yes we DO) right in the back yard. It's so convenient to put on my workout clothes, head to the yard, and be able to finish a whole body routine without leaving home. Aerobics, resistance training, stretching, power lifting, the whole nine yards, honey. And as an added benefit, I can do my tanning at the same time.

Of course you can't be fit outside without being fit inside as well- you KNOW it's true, it was just on Oprah. And good eating requires that you use only the BEST foods.

Thanks to our seasonal produce incubator, we have fruit and veggies that are fresh as can be and sometimes even enhanced with important trace minerals! And we have the latest technology for producing and keeping our milk and eggs at their peak freshness thanks to individual climate-controlled storage units that manufacture and hold these commodities till just before we use them.

There are times when we have just TOO MUCH food, if you can believe it, and then we employ our antiseptic pressure edibles sealer, which is absolutely fabulous since we can control the fat, salt and sugar amounts in the finished dishes, not to mention how darlingly festive all those pretty jars are lined up on the kitchen shelves.

And our son is simply thriving in this environment!

We decided not to enroll him in public school and he's enjoying the luxury of one on one tutoring. I KNOW it seems a horrible extravagance, but it's such a joy to see him blossoming with lesson plans that are authored specifically for him.

Well of COURSE he is involved in organized sports- every day after lessons are finished, he joins up with other kids in the neighborhood and participates in non-age level specific cross-cultural execution of a variety of casual competitions that encourage team play, foster both leadership and listening skills, and emphasize lasting friendships over short-term victory."

By this time, my audience is usually frozen with professionally whitened teeth exposed and drying out by their 'polite smiles', framed with their carefully painted and pouty lips. Their eyes (expertly lined and lashed with extensions) gaze at me a little glazedly, and I can tell they are not sure how to respond.

Since timing is everything, I never wait for their response. I'll wait till just before the silence gets plumb uncomfortable, smile even bigger and more sincere than THEIR smiles, graciously tell them how WONDERFUL it is seeing them again, how they simply MUST call me soon and come out to visit, and beat a hasty retreat to the food table (if there's anything left that's still edible) on my way out the door.

Between the door and my car, my shoes will be off.

Once in the car, the makeup gets rubbed away before it suffocates my face.

Home is calling me, and I hum a little ditty as I maneuver through the traffic towards my old Bubba truck with the gun rack, drafty old farmhouse, loveable serious Pyrenees in the yard, barnyard full of building and repair projects, vegetable garden, dairy goats, laying hens, old trusty pressure canner, and my beloved home schooled boy who's playing a never ending constantly shifting set of hybrid sports with the neighbor kids.

The public relations guys are right.

It's all in the 'spin'.

Drawing a Circle in the Sand- Teaching Awareness to A Consumer Society

The following is a true story. Names have not been changed to protect the innocent.

On a picnic one fine day several years ago, my son Alec and I were lunching with my friend Mary Helen and her twin boys James and Noah, also my son's age. Approximate age of these boys at the time is right around four years old.

My son was busy munching his Happy Meal and took a moment out from ingestion of grease and preservatives to inquire if the liquid in the wax carton was cows milk or goats milk. I told him it was cows milk and he accepted that without comment.

My friend's boys however, were suddenly very quiet and eyeing their wax cartons with grave suspicion.

"What do you mean, what KIND of milk???" they asked Alec.

Alec cheerfully explained. "The milk at OUR house is goats milk. Every morning my mom goes out and feeds the goats. Then she gets down on the ground next to them and milks them like this (insert visual of young boy doing realistic rendering of milking a goat). She brings it into the house, strains it and puts it in the fridge for us to drink."

After a stony silence, James announced, "Well, OUR milk comes from the STORE".

Alec allowed that most people do not have goats in their yard and that for the unfortunate masses; store-bought cows milk is the only sad alternative for a calcium-laden drink. James and Noah were STILL not happy, saying that THEIR milk does NOT come from COWS, it comes from the STORE.

In the manner of most pre-school and congressional discussions, this rapidly escalated to fisticuff status.

Now, Mary Helen is a veterinarian and these boys are exposed to many animals both in and out of 'nature' all the time. The Circle of Life is not a stranger to them. Or so she thought…

At James's pronouncement, followed by the zealous statement of belief, and the impending physical assault, Mary Helen was alarmed, and rose to the occasion with alacrity.

"WAIT- you are ALL right!" she hollered, the scruff of one boy in each hand, while I held my combatant at bay also. She then detailed how the cows milk that is usually in THEIR Sippy cups goes from the cow, to the automatic milking machine, into a truck with a lot of other cows' milk from a lot of other farms, to the factory to be cleaned up, sterilized and cartoned ready to be delivered to their local store. That's the point where they become personally involved with said milk. From cows. And that Alec spoke truth when he told them where HIS milk comes from.

Once the light of righteous indignation left the eyes of the three boys, they were loosed to resume their meal in silence. James and Noah would have nothing more to do with their milk.

I whispered to Mary Helen "Just wait till they learn that eggs come out of chickens' butts- they'll never eat another egg".

She blanched and looked a little faint.

Americans have always been farmers. Most of our founding fathers had huge farms and spent at least as much time in the fields and barns as thinking up Important Documents to sign. Then something happened.

We moved off of the farms in droves- driven by emancipation, drought, depression, disillusionment, the siren call of the cities who were hungry for manpower to run the ever-larger factories and accompanying businesses. Obviously this factory-workin' thing was not a cushy gig by any stretch of the imagination, but the promise of weekly wages that relied on your ability to get to work and do your job instead of your life resting on whether Mother Nature rained on your crops or not was a welcome relief to many.

A fundamental drive of the human soul is the wish that your children have a better life than you do. In the urban world, the way to a better life lay NOT in going back to the land, but to college for an advanced education. When the children of these factory workers reached their teens they did NOT swing BACK, they swung forward.

Teachers, lawyers, doctors, dentists, art history majors, mechanical and aerospace engineers began rolling off of the collegiate assembly lines like the Buicks and Frigidares that their fathers made.

This puts the average American at least two generations off of the land.

So what the heck does all that have to do with James, Noah and Alec dukin' it out over the source of their moo juice?

Somewhere in all this mess we call 'advancement', we not only abandoned the rural ways, we learned to shun them as well.

Clone-like orbs of vegefection that taste as interesting as they look have replaced fresh veggies from the garden, still warm from the sun and as individually scarred and lopsided as we are. Small details like vitamin content and flavor have been cast aside for uniformity, toughness under shipping stress, and shelf life. The veggies we buy at the supermarket have been genetically altered, chemically fertilized, drowned in pesticide, power-washed and dunked in wax, but thank GOD they aren't DIRTY.

Meats (actually chickens, pigs and cows- who KNEW?) are grown in horrendous conditions and fed enough steroids to make them grow fast and enough antibiotics to keep them alive till we kill them. Of course 'we' does not technically refer to 'us', because 'we' don't really want to see them till they are killed, gutted, soaked in anti-bacterial preservatives, hosed mostly off and wrapped in shrink wrap. They aren't really animals anymore then, they are tenders, chops and steaks. Cuz eating dead animals would be gross.

"We get milk from cows and eggs from chickens" is our standard line to children. Are we even aware that when they put a picture to this statement they most likely get a mental image of various barnyard animals in white coats, manning the assembly lines in the milk and egg factories?

And let's look for a moment at the other end of things.

There's a most magical vehicle that comes into your neighborhood on a regular basis. You can hear it from blocks away by the sound it makes. People run out of their houses to meet it. People look forward to its coming. People are very sad when they miss it, and some have actually been known to chase it down in their cars. By your smile I know you know what I am talking about.

Ice cream? Who said anything about **ice cream**?

I'm talking about the garbage truck, silly.

That phantasmal chariot that swallows our trash like a giant metal pelican and carries it off. Poof. It's gone. If a child is precocious enough to ask, "Mommy, where is the garbage truck taking our stinky putrefied wastes?" the answer will be "to the dump, honey", and that will be the end of it.

Our food comes from the store and our wastes go to the dump.

The Circle of Life has been replaced with the Tunnel Vision of Consumerism.

We need to take our precious children and challenge them. If they stop asking 'why?' we are lost. "Why?" must be answered, and then “Before that?” and “Then what?” need to be addressed as well.

“We get our food from the store” must be followed with “But BEFORE that- it comes from the factory and BEFORE that it was grown and harvested on the farm using compost in the soil to help it grow”. If any link in that chain includes anything that we are ashamed of or don’t want our children knowing (or ingesting) we must change it, either by demanding that changes are made, or by growing our own.

“Our trash go to the dump” must be followed with “And AFTER that, it goes into landfill which takes up huge amounts of land area and pollute the earth, air and water. We must make sure that our additions to the landfill are minimum by recycling what we can, composting what we can, reusing what we can, and then and only then, throwing the rest away in biodegradable bags, not those quilted plastic nightmares that are advertised to be able to stop a runaway train.

Ashes to ashes, dust-to-dust, compost to compost, everything goes around and around in a circle as old as the earth itself.

Traveling in a straight line is exciting in a brash, blazing a trail kind of way. Taming of the wilderness (natural or corporate) and all that. The future is unknown, and there is no past before your tiny self-appearing on the scene. If you are a proper consumer, you are also teaching your children to grow up blazing their own trail.

Taking what you need where you find it and discarding after use is unsustainable, irresponsible and ultimately discouraging. Because no matter how hard we try to hide it behind and underneath chemically processed hair, botoxed faces, designer-clad bodies that have been liposuctioned into submission, encased in our autos thundering down the highway with our cell phones attached to our ears there is still a core of organic matter right in the center of our souls, that little core needs roots, and roots need compost, dangit.

The Circle of Life requires a lot more thought and care to travel than a straight line, because it's a CIRCLE and you will be back around this way again. Judicious pruning and mulching must replace slash and burn. Attention is required to preserve the knowledge and cornerstones of the past both for use today, and for our children's' use in the future.
The child who finds an egg, sees that egg hatch into a chick, feeds that chick till it grows and lays eggs of it's own has learned a valuable lesson.

Planting seeds together, watering, weeding, playing in the dirt in general, harvesting and eating something you planted together will make an impression that will last long after the last cucumber is pickled.

Helping at milking time early in the morning has its payoff later in the day with homemade chocolate ice cream.

It's our duty as homesteaders to not only keep our own family and farm in order, but to teach others how to do the same, because our 'family' is everyone and our 'farm' is this whole planet.

Quietly, gently, patiently, one perfect free-range egg, soft juicy taste bud tingling tomato and fresh cranked bowl of ice cream at a time, we can and will ease this generation out of the long dark Tunnel of Consumerism and back into the grandmotherly hug that is the Circle of Life.

Paying Attention- the Most Important Skill on Your Farm

In the grand scheme of acquiring, establishing and running your homestead, you will be paying A LOT of people.

You'll be paying the sellers of the land, the bank you get your loan from, the county for various (and seemingly endless) permits, contractors, insurance people, moving people, utility people, livestock sellers, your friends and family (although you can usually get by with paying these in either food or beer…), and there will be many many days when you will feel like having a good shrink on retainer would be money well spent.

But all the above will be wasted effort and cash if you don't follow the most important rule- Pay Attention.

We now live in a society where anyone living in even remotely 'modern' digs is literally overloaded with mental, visual and audio stimuli. If you are like most people- take this little test.

Stop.

Close your eyes.

Listen.

What do you hear?

Computer running, of course. TV on somewhere? MORE than one TV on somewhere? Radio or CD player? Refrigerator? Furnace or air conditioning? Kids playing (fighting)? Dogs barking? Traffic outside?

What's the first thing you notice if the power goes out? (After the DARK…)

It's

So

Quiet.

Take driving. Think of everything you must keep track of, visually and audibly. Now add the stuff we do on TOP of that- talk to passengers, referee the kids in the back seat, answer the phone, eat, drink, and sing along with the radio… It's amazing anyone gets anywhere alive.

Personally, I can't stand noise. At work, it's quiet. No radio, no music. Just quiet. Same at home if I'm here by myself. I use the vacuum cleaner under the greatest of duress cuz it's just too dang LOUD. I've made a rule to my video-lovin' boys that they can have ONE thing on at a time- no playing a computer game while watching something on the tube. Makes me insane. Our new place has no cable TV connections, and I refuse to get satellite. We will have one local station, and PBS. Ahhhhh…better.

Kids born anytime after about 1970 or so grew up in front of the color TV. From an early age they have had images and sounds paraded in front of them without having to do anything more strenuous than blinking. Once these kids got to school, school was boring. So schools had to keep up. Short, fast lessons that jump from one thing to another is the norm, because these little people just don't have an attention span any longer than it takes to get from one commercial break to the next. THEN they go to Chuck E Cheese for relaxing entertainment. I hate Chuck E Cheese. Place makes me all twitchy and I have to take a migraine pill 20 minutes before entering…

What does ANY of this have to do with farming???

Just this. Somewhere in the last 30 years or so, we lost our ability to Pay Attention. We too often rely on someone else to tell us how or what to think or how to do things, and exchanging 'virtual life' for real life. A good example of this was my (ex) husband watching the Sunday morning fishing shows religiously. On beautiful Sunday mornings, I'd see him in front of the TV, taking NOTES on the type of line/bait/lure to use and when/how to fish. I'd look out the window at the lovely day and think how pretty the sunshine was sparkling off of the LAKE that was less than 300 ft from our door, where his tackle box quietly collected dust. Insanity.

Going out for the day? Better check the weather channel to see what it's gonna do. Of course you could also LOOK OUT THE WINDOW. Crazy.

Once you get onto the farm, it's a different story. There are no indicator lights on livestock, or little printed directions on each sprout in the garden.

You will have to Pay Attention.

Having every piece of equipment or tool you could ever use will not help you if you don't keep it clean, dry, maintained and somewhere you can find it when you need it.

Every time you feed your livestock, pay attention to the feed. Is it fresh smelling? Do they have access to plenty of good clean water? How does each and every one of your critters look? Are they standing funny? Moving slower than usual? Coughing, sniffling, panting, having normal stools? Are they too fat, or too skinny? All of the animals we use as livestock are pretty far down on the food chain, and if you remember your National Geographic specials, they will APPEAR healthy till they are pretty much dead. This keeps them from being singled out of the herd and into the predator buffet until it's a certainty that they are not going to get well. Therefore, once your animal looks obviously ailing, it's gonna be a long row to hoe to get it healthy, if it can be done at all.

Now, the above is not nearly as time consuming as you'd think, even if you have livestock numbering in the hundreds. Remember the first few times you drove a car (or the last time you tried it impaired in some way). Staring at the steering wheel, belted in, mentally checking off every little step to turning on the vehicle and getting onto the road. Of course, now you do it without thinking (starting the car, not driving impaired- that's BAD- don't do it), and the same will be true about checking your stock. After just a short while, your head and eyes will be checking stock while the rest of you is engaged otherwise. Any little variation from 'normal' will stop you in your tracks.

The same holds true for your garden. Check every little plantlet every day. Are they green and happy looking? Are they wilty? Turning brown? Fuzzy looking? Do you see bugs on them (even a few- since there is truly no such thing as 'a few bugs')? Catching a problem early is vital to gardening success since you can lose an entire crop literally overnight if defensive measures are not taken immediately (I prove this to myself year after year after year…)

Being in tune with the weather when you have a homestead is much more than tucking an umbrelly into your car on your way to work. Most of the work to be done on a farm is outside. Your individual climate will teach you when you need to do things. Learning to work when it's the cool part of the day in the summer and the warm part of the day in the winter will save your patience, your sanity and your health, and again, once you've done it awhile deliberately, you will naturally adjust your schedule. As if by magic, your day will flow from inside to out with the temperature (without one look at the Weather Channel), and one day you will wake up JUST BECAUSE IT'S MORNING, and not when the alarm clock sounds.

Congratulations- you are a homesteader.

I think our society has it backwards. The assumption is that because our brains are so big, and capable of processing and storing so much information, that we need to throw huge amounts of data at it at all times to keep us 'sharp'. Bigger, brighter, louder, is better in such an ever-growing cacophony of sense-numbing images and sounds that it's a wonder we aren't all on the ground having sensory overload seizures.

Maybe, just maybe

Our brains are large to be able to soak up details. Tiny little things that make a huge difference to our lives and our souls.

I have a seven-year-old son. This boy is a whirling dervish of constant motion and noise. During the day I see him mostly just out of my line of vision, speeding from one activity to the next. The world is a gigantic treasure chest crying out for discovery, and a mere mother cannot get in the way. Ah, but at night, when the day has taken it's toll on the boy and he's fought sleep as long as possible and finally fallen in a heap to dream of dragons and pirates, he's there for me to see. Not just to check if he's covered, or taken some sort of amphibian to bed with him, but to see. Every parent knows what I mean. You sit on the edge of the bed, in the quiet murk of night and you etch every line of that face into your memory- the freckles, the terminal bed head, the chin and eyebrows so like his father's, every detail. And I defy any parent to deny bending forward in the dark and inhaling the scent of their offspring's head- clean from the bath, or still filled with sunshine and sand from the day's adventures, that too is driven into your memory base. Because the details are what you hold onto not only during his waking hours when he's traveling so fast all you catch is a blur, but forever.

Life is in the details.

Too much of life denies the details. We're too busy, we're late, and we can't waste TIME.

My daughter lives and works in Washington DC and recently sent me an article. I'll add the link to the bottom if you'd like to read it for yourself. The Post did a little experiment to find out just how imprisoned within our own busy-ness we all are. They got a world-class violinist to set up wearing blue jeans and a t-shirt in the Metro- his open violin case for tips normally holds his Stradivarius violin. He did not play popular tunes that may have niggled someone's brain enough for them to pause- he played classical pieces. Beautiful classical pieces by a world-class violinist playing a priceless instrument.

A few paused. A few tossed some coins into his case without even slowing down. Most didn't even look. An artist whose concerts sell out at over $100 per seat collected $37 plus change during rush hour in our nation's capitol.

This is part of the wonderment of living a rural lifestyle. While a lot of the world is planning for the future, today slips away, never to return. A homesteader must be intimately familiar with the present, or lose everything and be left with no future. And once your brain is trained to look for details instead of the grand expanses, your horizons are limitless.

You can't check your goats without smiling at the kids frolicking. You can't eye your chickens without studying their social order. Try to examine your garden without smelling the earth. Mentally noting the position of the sun leaves you looking directly at the clouds (and yes, that one DOES look like a bunny).

Paying attention to the details does not exclude planning for the future; it encompasses our plans for the future. For we are planning not only for our families, and ourselves but also for everything in our care- up to and including the very land we are living on. Every decision is weighed and thought through with attention to the details of the co-operation of everything and everyone that decision will affect.

Because that's what we do- we co-habitate, co-mingle and co-operate our homesteads with literally millions of other living things, most of them not just benign, but absolutely integral to the fate of our endeavors.

“"For the want of a nail, the shoe was lost; for the want of a shoe the horse was lost; and for the want of a horse the rider was lost, being overtaken and slain by the enemy, all for the want of care about a horseshoe nail."
 -- Benjamin **Franklin**

On your homestead, paying attention to details will decrease what you will have to pay to the Veterinarian, the hardware store, and people to come in to fix something that got mucked up due to negligence. The physical safety and well being of your place is reason enough to train yourself to hone in on the details.

Learning to absorb the peripheral images, sounds, textures and aromas is gravy.

And everyone loves gravy.

(The aforementioned article) http://www.washingtonpost.com/wp-dyn/content/article/2007/04/04/AR2007040401721.html

Gotta Getta Ger- The Permanent Temporary Movable Structure

We have the land.

We have a house we are selling.

Our next step is to move all our stuff and us over TO the land and build our home.

Although we love to camp, and in recent history here in Texas, we could lay out all of our stuff in the naked meadow after June 1st without fear of a raindrop touching it before October, some sort of shelter seems prudent.

*This article is not about LIVING in a Ger (yurt), but about the choosing, research and shopping end of the process. The assemblage and living part will be another story…

Unless you have found a place with a home already on it (my last two homesteads have been one of these), or have a lot of money lying idle and can afford to build your new house while living in your old house (I've heard some people can actually do this, although no one in my social circle can claim such high finance), you'll be faced with the dilemma of where to live in the 'between time'.

Mainstream Americans put most of their stuff in storage and either rent a place for the 6-8 months it takes for their builder to put up their house, or buy a little mobile home and set it out yonder while the builder does his thing then have it hauled off when they are done. A few daring folks will live in a camper, and a few will move in with relatives.

None of these options are open to us because
-No one in their right mind would rent to someone with over 100 critters

-Mobile homes come equipped with things like appliances and kitchen counters- things we are bringing with us and it would be redundant to put ours in storage while paying for theirs
-We don't have access to a camper and with our health issues and the time it will take to build our permanent house, more room and comfort will be necessary to keep a semblance of sanity
-We really want to maintain good relations with our relations. This requires a respectful distance at all times.

And our plans are to build our permanent house. Not "hire a builder, choose a plan and pick out colors and faucets" kind of building. More of a "design it out on graph paper, accumulate the supplies, learn and assemble as we go" sort of building. So our timeline is a little different. My conservative estimate is five years from start to finish- paying as we go. Granted, life may get in the way of this plan and cause it to be amended, but that's the plan today, and we're sticking to it.

After hearing "So what're ya'll gonna do? Live in a tent?" for the thousandth time from friends and acquaintances, Ward looked at me and said, "You know, I've always thought yurts were neat".

Thus began "Yurt Quest".

(Adding- being very aware that we are, in fact, sitting front row/center of Tornado Alley, we will not be moving into our yurt without first having in place a storm shelter. We may be eccentric, but we ain't crazy)

Yurts are the traditional homes of nomadic tribes who make their livelihood following their flocks across a forbidding landscape. A yurt is designed to be a permanent, movable home, which only sounds contradictory. The original yurts (Mongolian Gers) are assembled from local materials (saplings, cotton cloth and lots and lots of felted wool) and have been fine tuned over the last 3000 years or so to be cool in the hot summer sun, warm in the frigid winters, and stay upright and strong through the flat line winds coming from the steppes.

Here in the US, yurts have been adjusted, updated and built large scale by three companies- Pacific Yurts (http://www.yurts.com/what/default.aspx), Ranier (http://www.rainieryurts.com/), and Colorado Yurts (http://www.coloradoyurt.com/).

All three come recommended by actual American yurt-dwellers as having quality products and very good to excellent customer service.

After looking at all three sites, and using the handy (and fun) price quote estimators, I called both Ranier and Pacific, whose friendly sales staff sent out informative packets. The packet from Pacific was more in depth and flashier, so being a creature drawn to such things, (and the fact that their yurts priced out as less expensive), I've been working with and talking to Scott at Pacific to get the Yurt of Our Dreams.

The yurts built by one of the above companies are sleek, clean-lined, and beautiful in simplicity- unlikely yet wonderful crosses of "Girl Scout Sleepover Camp Platform Tent" and "Yuppie Renovated Warehouse on the River Loft". They use state of the art materials to ensure a non-leaking, comfortable, very livable space that is as strong as something made mainly of cloth can be.

I was happy. I had a plan. I knew what I was doing.

Then my friend Dawn skipped in and ruined it all.

It came as an innocent looking email titled "Look at THESE".

And my world tilted flat off of its orbit.

Gers. Authentic Mongolian Gers made by Authentic Mongolians. And importable to the US.

Where the US Yurt is sleek, a Mongolian Ger is touchable- like a teddy bear. They are decorated outside by embroidery around the doorway and inside by each…and…every…rafter being painted with elaborate designs and set off by carvings which match the carvings on the door and toono (circular opening at the top of the roof). The wood is painted in bright colors, which is appealing to me. The outer cloth, inner cloth and felting are really cloth and felt, which is appealing to me. The fact that the Mongolian Ger- made and painted to order in the same way they've been made for thousands of years is CHEAPER even shipped from the other side of the planet than the ones made in a factory in Oregon is WILDLY appealing to me.

So I contacted three companies selling 'Authentic Mongolian Ger' and got a response from one of them (http://www.mongolyurt.mn/en/yourtegb.html#yurt). Heloise Rey is very helpful and patient, sending a lot of pictures and answering all my questions to the best of her abilities.

I also joined a yahoo group (http://groups.yahoo.com/group/The_Yurt_Community/), and was instantly embroiled in the (previously unknown to me) vicious war between 'traditional' and 'modern' yurt/ger owners.

Traditional ger enthusiasts say that the US made yurts are flimsy, plastic mutations of a time tested and loved building form. They say if a yurt is not surrounded by felt, it's not a yurt- it's a tent. And there's nothing wrong with a tent- just don't call it a yurt. They say that if a yurt is built with solid walls and windows, it's not a yurt- it's a round house. And there's nothing wrong with a round house- just don't call it a yurt. A traditional ger's lattice is it's bones, and the felt is it's muscle- stabilizing and holding the ger intact in wind storms so they don't need 'snow and wind kit' add ons like the modern ones. A traditional ger stands on the ground- solid earth beneath it (covered with rugs), natural wood and wool on the sides and the sky open through the toono. One door. No windows (although the Mongolian companies will add them to appeal to the American market). Traditionally, air is circulated by simply rolling up part of the side, causing the cooler air on the ground to ooze in and rise up and out the toono as it gets warmer. The door is solid wood, sometimes bracketed by narrow windows; decoration and carvings showing the status of its occupants. Inside, the placement of furniture and living areas are strictly adhered to from ger to ger. This ger is made to be taken down in a few hours' time, strapped to the back of a yak, and re-built in the same amount of time at the new grazing grounds.

Modern yurt enthusiasts say that the traditional gers are poorly made imports and fall apart in our climate. They say that the felt gets moldy and attracts bugs and mice. They extol the strength of their airline cable tie-downs, beauty of having windows all around, ease of care of the waterproof poly/vinyl exterior, and snug their yurts down on wooden platforms that are everything from a deck a foot above ground, to way high up in a tree- but they MUST be placed on a deck. They can be simple one-room shelters or homes with electric/plumbing, partition walls and (in the bigger ones) loft living areas. With the wind and snow kits attached, they are as stable in high winds as a lot of brand new mobile homes (rated for up to 90mph). The modern yurt can be taken down at the end of summer/hunting season in a few hours time, strapped to the luggage rack of your minivan, and stored in the garage till next year OR lived in full time- in my cyber-wanderings, the longest yurt dweller I've come across has been living in her Pacific yurt with her family in Minnesota quite comfortably for seven years. In the US made yurts, insulation is provided by a 'reflective medium' that looks like bubble wrap coated with tin foil. Although the manufacturers claim that it works by reflecting the heat OUT in the summer and IN in the winter, the real life yurt dwellers have given mixed reviews. I've looked at alternatives to the bubble-stuff, from natural fiber insulation sheets made of recycled cotton/denim to recycled plastic heat-bonded to Styrofoam on rolls, and heard of folks using everything from straw stuffed in-between layers to garage sale blankets sewn to the sides.

Then there's a whole NUTHER faction who builds their own…

It boggles the mind.

With my eyes and brain slightly crossed, I've attempted to figure out not what's 'right', but what's right for my family in my climate and in my circumstances.

To their credit, not a single resource person on either side of the Yurt Debate has been outright demeaning to the other side. They just think their side is better, and have told me why, calmly and rationally. It's been great fun and wonderfully educational to talk to people from Oregon to Mongolia to New York City to Holland to Spain, and I'll happily share what I've found out.

Although Mongolia can get very hot, very cold and very windy, it's very dry (it's in the Gobi desert- guess I slept through that class…), and the materials used to make the traditional gers are not grown or made in or made FOR a damp environment. The other side of the planet is very far away, and your average Mongolian cannot comprehend the humidity of East Texas, just as I did not realize that Mongolia was arid. As mentioned before, Heloise in Mongolia did answer my questions, but admitted while doing so that these answers were to the best of HER knowledge, not necessarily what WOULD happen when the ger was assembled and exposed to this climate. What I've gathered is that when the imported ger meets the southern American humidity, the glue has issues, the paint has issues, the felt has issues, and the material has issues. This does not mean they are 'cheap imports', it means they are built for and in a different environment.

Now, there are people in Europe (and if you join the yurt yahoo group, you will meet them), who are making 'traditional Mongolian ger' using the measurements and structure of Mongolian gers but with materials that will hold up to a more humid environment. But again, there's still a big ol' pond between Europe and here, and the gentleman I talked to in Holland (Froit- nice man, very helpful and patient) couldn't comprehend WHY I need my ger to be tight sealed on the bottom. I don't mind it being on the ground, but crawlie things shouldn't be able to get in. He suggested we get a cat. Apparently, things like poisonous spiders; scorpions and snakes (not to mention skeeters as big as a fry pan) are not a problem in Holland. He also stressed that a ger needs to (as in MUST) be moved at least every six months for its health. And the wait time on one of these 'improved traditional European gers' is right at or just over six months.

IF we were not needing this structure to sit securely in place for at least five years, and IF we didn't have health and comfort requirements to consider, we'd happily wait for a traditional ger. In fact, at some point in the future, I'd love to get a small one to be a little 'retreat' we would move around from one 'favorite spot' to another- from the top of the hill, to the creek bank, to the back high corner overlooking the marsh, etc. depending on the season.

But that's not what we need right now.

Which brings us right back into the lap of Scott at Pacific Yurts, who did not hold my brief fling with the Mongolian ger against me. In fact, he helpfully admitted that if we wanted to stencil decorations over the doors/windows, we could use latex house paint without compromising the integrity of the waterproofing. And that the wooden parts come oiled, not varnished, and would hold any oil-based decorative painted designs we might want to add to them. Now if I could only get him to carve a dragon into the front door….

Natural Building Colloquium- Kerrville TX
Getting Down and Dirty with Mother Nature

If you are thinking and have been reading about Alternative Building styles, this is one of those things that you see on the 'net and think to yourself "Golly, that would be SO much fun. We should go." Then you see that it's being held (insert somewhere that's clearly too far from home to be affordable or sensible). Deep depressed sigh, and the conviction that SOMEDAY…

And then one comes up that's tantalizingly near to home, and it's sorely tempting. Being a Grown-Up and all, the excuses NOT to go pop up like Whack-a-Moles-
-It's too expensive
-We'd have to take time off of work
-It's too expensive
-It's too hard to leave the farm for a weekend
-It's too expensive

Here's where the decision must be made to keep dreaming, or to get dirty.

The Natural Building Colloquium was held in Kerrville TX on a perfect autumn weekend. We went, and we got dirty.

Having had a number of family challenges this past year that all involved fistfuls of cash being thrown at them, our discretionary budget glowed as red as Rudolph's nose, so that's what we decided- this weekend would be our Christmas present to ourselves.

Once I put down on paper the stuff we'd be learning, the people we'd be meeting and the helpful contacts we'd be making, even if we only learned ONE thing that would save us time, energy and money, that ONE thing would most likely cover the expense of the weekend.

And I didn't have to gift wrap it. Sweet.

This is a totally factual account of the first weekend of the Natural Building Colloquium as experienced by one tiny family- I am confident that every other participant has a completely different story- there was THAT much going on.

But if you've never been to one- it'll give you an inkling of what to expect.

Or not.

Because I'm sure they are all as different as snowflakes.

The setting was perfect- a 50-acre campground in the heart of the Central Texas Hill Country. And the weather was outstanding- overcast to keep it from getting uncomfortably hot during the day, and just chilly enough at night to make for good snuggling in the outdoor theater during the evening presentations. We were in a drought condition, so there were no campfires, and that was a disappointment to my son Alec, aged 7, who was looking forward to blazing marshmallows, but for most of the tasks at hand, it was ideal.

The days began with food- wonderful, fresh food made on site and eaten in the Great Outdoors- tasty, unique, colorful. Alec made it to the end of the serving counter the first morning, stopped, turned to me suspiciously and asked, “Where's the MEAT???”

Oh yeah. Sorry hon., this is a vegetarian shindig. After the initial shock/panic attack, he managed to find items that were not only ingestible, but also deemed “really not bad”. In case you have never had children- “really not bad” is as high a compliment as you should expect when introducing something ‘strange’ into their diets.

After breakfast was Morning Circle- in the amphitheatre set into the hillside. Announcements, schedule affirmations and changes, and some songs and silliness to start the day.

Then on to talks, demonstrations and projects.

This type of event really should be attended by multiple folks in each group- there is so much going on at once; it's the only way to glean even a portion of knowledge. At any given moment, my husband would be at a demonstration, I would be in a discussion group, and our son would be wallowing in some sort of earth/straw/water concoction.

And that's one of the first things that struck me about this gathering- most of the time if you bring your child/children to workshops or meetings, a good part of your energy is spent telling them to "shhhhhhhhh" and "please sit still" and "YACKKKK! Don't do/touch that!!!" From the very first moments here- in the breakfast line Saturday morning- Alec was looked on as an equal member of the gathering and he and the woman in front of us were trying to out-do each other by bending various body parts in directions they were clearly not designed to bend. (He won, but only by virtue of his age and the fact that his young bones and joints aren't completely 'cemented in place' yet). Every project we attended, the first thing he'd ask was "What can I do to help?" and every single project leader gave him something that was clearly truly helpful- not 'something to amuse the kid while the grownups do the work'.

Of course building with natural materials is generally a messy, non-exacting science, but that's what attracts THIS grownup to it anyhow- I'm much better at getting messy and being non-exacting than being bent over delicate precision work.

The Colloquium took place over a 10-day period, and we attended a mere 2. For information on the entire schedule and list of presenters, check out http://www.naturalbuildingtexas.org/

Here's what this family saw and did-

A demonstration on cob building took place in the children's play area of the campground, where they built a wall/bench/thatched roof over the sandbox. We were able to participate in the wall building, which was great fun and attracted most of the children present to stomp the mixture and slap it onto the pile-that-became-a-wall.

A new staff building was being constructed out of hay bales, and across the road from the staff building they made the trusses out of salvage pallets.

The entrance to the campground was being spiffied up with a cob, earth bag and adobe combo sign holding hut, with hand peeled cedar posts.

Recycle bin shelters were being made in the meadow out of bamboo.

And then, Alec saw the adobe.

That's pretty much the last we saw of him all weekend. Really. After the Colloquium it took some careful chiseling and several showers to get beneath the adobe and back down to the 'boy layer'. Patt Taylor, overseeing that section, works with groups of school-aged youngsters in his renovation projects in the Southwest and Mexico, and adopted Alec as his right-hand-man.

It seems that straw bale building is the new 'thing', and most of the people there were geared towards that form of housing. We attended the areas we are personally interested in- building with earth, and collecting/storing/treating water. I don't know why I just can't get 'into' the whole straw bale thing- I think it's a tiny vestige of the "Three Little Pigs" story juxtaposed next to the fact that we live in Tornado Alley that cause some sort of disharmonious clash in my brain.

I admit, I have a weird brain, but it's the only one I was dealt, so there ya go.

The talks we attended were extremely well done- and it's refreshingly obvious that the speakers are not 'professional lecturers'. They speak zealously, passionately, their words flowing through the air not to convey learned knowledge, but straight from their own hearts into yours.

We were encouraged by the quiet earnestness of Patt Taylor discussing the renovation/salvation of adobes that are simultaneously strong as the ages are long and appallingly fragile in the face of human stupidity, and Art Ludwig sharing with us his ideas about water- not as a preacher, not as a profiteer, but sharing what works for HIS family and HIS little corner of Mother Earth, and what may work for our families in our corners as well.

We were intrigued and challenged to think out of the box by the 'and now for something completely different' ideas of Tom Watson, who pioneered the 'Watson Wick' and other novel ways to deal with gray and black water.

We were brought to tears by Carole Menkes, surrounded by her husband's achingly beautiful pieces of bamboo art, sharing his work with us a mere 4 days after his unexpected death; she told us that even though his memorial service would be on the Monday following, she considered THIS moment her memorial to him- in the midst of people who care about and appreciate beautiful natural things, with the gentle breeze carrying the songs of the earth through the pavilion. She never did refer to Mark in the past tense, and that was fitting, for I'm certain that he WAS there.

And we were completely taken with and entertained by the lively stylings of Brad Lancaster, who taught us about rainwater catchment using jokes, songs, and complete groaners of puns- all the while leaping from one end of the stage to the other.

We were most looking forward to meeting The Earth bag People- Doni and Kaki, since we are planning on using earth bags extensively on our new place. Unfortunately, they were stranded in Utah with car trouble and didn't make it to Kerrville before we had to leave, which was disappointing, but sort of out of anyone's control.

The only 'landed on the wrong planet' moment of the weekend was the Builders' Forum, led by David Eisenberg. Apparently, even in this group, 'Owner-Builder' means you hire an architect, get a mittful of permits and utilize people like electricians, plumbers, and contractors. I showed up with our plans on graph paper, hoping to get pointers and ideas on how a big guy with health concerns, a pear shaped old hippiechick and a 7 year old boy can physically put together a comfy, earth-friendly residence using shovels, leverage and salvage-gleanings, and the first three subjects covered were- zoning, financing, and insurance. Go figure. Normally, I would not have been afraid to interject my own questions, but the time allotted was limited, and most of the attendees needed to know about what was already on the table, so I approached David afterwards and he was very supportive and is willing to give us pointers and whatnot as we do our actual building.

Not a problem for me personally, as I am terminally 'time challenged', but worth mentioning, is that the times listed on the Day's Schedule board were at best Loose Suggestions. Hey. Creativity, learning and thinking defy rigidity.

At the opening Morning Circle, we were encouraged to make a Prayer Flag sometime during our stay- they hung these multicolored butterflies of thought all around the amphitheatre- waving jewels of emotion and dreams. Alec sat long with his ink pen, staring at the blank piece of cloth, before his heart told his fingers what I feel is the epitome of why we were there-

Our homes are shelters for our bodies, and safe places for our 'stuff'. As residents of Mother Earth, if we are fortunate enough to have the opportunity to build our own, we should try our level best to practice the following-

-Use the smallest amount of materials as possible

-Use natural and/or salvaged materials wherever we can

-If we must cause disruption by our building and living, to make sure it's as tiny as it can be, and to compensate Mother Earth's other residents accordingly

-Build using as many passive/alternative sources of power as we can- always remembering that eliminating things that NEED power is the most effective savings
-Strive for self-contained food and water systems, stressing local plants and animals that don't require a lot of chemical intervention to produce well, and even if literally surrounded by fresh water, to cherish it- it's our greatest treasure

Our personal goal is to build by hand, quietly and slowly, using materials inherent to our region- earth, stone, and logs. A shelter should be as individual as the family that lives in it- 'houses' have Resale Value, 'homes' have Value Without Measure.

In our society "Everything has a price", but truly wealthy families know that some things are not for sale and are irreplaceable. People to love and who love us back cannot be bought, meaningful employment sometimes has no paycheck, and Home should welcome us and shelter us from whatever the rest of the human world throws at us.

What better escape is there from a culture full of speed, pointy things, plastic, mass production and noise than an embrace of earth, logs, straw, fiber and stone- every inch an individual spirit, formed with care by your own hands and the hands of your loved ones into one…big…giant…hug.

Natural building. An age-old idea whose time has come. Again.

RAISING CHICKENS FROM SCRATCH – WHICH CAME FIRST? THE CHICKEN OR THE EGG

The first livestock most new homesteaders bring home to the farm are chickens. And rightly so.

They're small, relatively harmless, provide both meat and eggs, and if they have to and are given the chance, they even rustle up their own grub (literally).

The majority of articles written about getting and keeping chickens start with "Buy your chicks", and describe the pros and cons of hatchery vs. feed store and hatchery vs. other hatchery. Of course you have to start somewhere, so for your FIRST round of chickens, this is the first step. Find chicks and purchase them.

If meat birds for yourself and for sale to others are what you are raising, they have a very limited lifespan before becoming a block on the food pyramid, and a lot of people prefer the breeds that are specifically used as dinner- Cornish X being the most popular. For a large amount of meat in a short amount of time, they really can't be beat.

If, however, your goal as a small homesteader is to have a flock of chickens for both meat and eggs, there are a number of 'dual purpose' breeds in an amazing array of colors (and that lay eggs in an amazing array of colors), and a lot of these birds have the added advantage of being prone to broodiness.

For your purposes, this is a good thing, and does not include heavy sighs, hoarding of chocolate, or tearful outbursts on the part of the hens. Broodiness in chickens is the tendency to WANT to sit (or set) on their own eggs, with the end result being more chickens.

Way back when, this is how chickens made more chickens.

Black Australorps (my personal favorites), Buff Orpingtons, Rhode Island Reds, Hampshire Reds, Speckled Sussex, Barred

Rocks and the Brahmas are among these dual-purpose breeds, although there are certainly others. These are the birds who made up the feathered backbone of the family farm- hens who laid eggs, sat on those eggs, hatched out and raised up several clutches of brand spankin' new poultry every year. These breeds are bulky enough (the reason they are referred to as Heavy Breeds) that the tiny roosters that get hatched out make darn good eating right before they become problematic teens.

Meat.
Eggs.
And repeat.

The ultimate renewable resource.

Somewhere along the line, egg production became commercialized and hens who 'went broody' became more of a bother than an asset- who wants to get bloodied every day when stealing a mother's offspring? Plus, all that extra weight and bulk just takes more feed to keep healthy. Thus, the advent of the White Leghorns (which look nothing at all like Foghorn Leghorn, unless Ol' Foghorn were to become anorexic and twitchy)- hens that are ADVERTISED as "Non-Setters"; in effect, bad mothers who drop an egg every single day, go on about their business and never look back.

The average dual purpose laying hen will lay an egg every day or so, for about 2 years. At that point, their production drops off and a lot of folks recommend making them all into stew and buying a fresh team.

But here's the thing.

At the end of that 2 years, my average broodiness-prone hen will have given me at LEAST two dozen more chickens, **AND** at LEAST 350 eggs. If I purchase my little chicks at $2 each, and eggs sell for $2 per dozen, that hen has provided me with over $100, while costing me…chicken feed, and precious little of that. Considering that my personal flock free ranges and I offer up hen scratch once a day but it's mostly ignored by them in favor of bugs, weeds and other stuff chickens were made to eat, my hens just retire here. They've earned it.

And if your flock is constantly being renewed from within, there won't BE a time when you have all Old Biddies.

Renewing the Flock the Easiest Way

Gather your initial flock. Some people prefer to get all one breed of chicken, and some like a feathery confetti look out in their yard. We have a yard full of confetti chickens, and each subsequent generation becomes more and more colorful. My initial chick order was like Saturday morning at Dunkin' Donuts. Over the phone I placed my minimum order of 25 chicks- "I'll take three of these, two of those, four of this other kind, and a little cream-filled one". Just kidding. You can only find cream-filled chicks at Easter time, and those are wrapped in colorful foil. I found out from that first order which breeds work in our situation (free ranging = attrition by coyote unless the birds are dark colored and very quick footed), and which ones…weren't.

My second order was something called the Ornamental Layer Collection, and I split the box of 25 chicks with a friend of mine. Among my dozen, I received 2 Aracaunas and an Egyptian Fayouma. These two breeds are not supposed to go broody, and the Aracaunas haven't, but we've forgiven them since they lay gorgeous greenish blue eggs. One day the little Fayouma disappeared, and I feared she'd been served up for coyote breakfast. I was surprised since she was the first to alarm when there were hungry predators about. I was even more surprised when she showed up one fine morning three weeks later with three chicklets behind her. Exceptions to the rule- I love 'em.

For hens to lay eggs, you don't need a rooster.
For hens to lay eggs that turn into more chickens, you do.

A good rooster is worth his weight in corn. He'll guard his hens, protect the chicks and eggs, and escort everyone back into the coop at night. The trick is to find one that will do all the above without viewing you (or your children) as the enemy. So far, my best rooster has been my Barred Rock/Hampshire Red, and my worst was a little Frizzle Bantam. Even within breeds, this will vary, as my first roo was a Light Brahma purchased because they were reported to be calm and gentle.

He made delicious soup.

Once hens and rooster are in place, it's just a matter of time before you have the magic of more chickens.

I collect eggs every day about lunchtime. I know all the movies show hens laying a nice warm egg at the crack of dawn, but mine are slothful. After sleeping in, rustling up a hearty breakfast and a few cups of coffee, they think about maybe laying an egg before lunchtime and Oprah.

When I first started with chickens, I built a beautiful bank of nesting boxes inside the coop. The chickens loved them. They slept in them. They scratched bugs out of them. They pooped on and in them. Never once did they lay an egg in them. Not once. They chose their own places to lay their eggs, and at any given time there are two or three spots all the hens will lay in. Periodically, apparently according to some Secret Chicken Calendar, the hens will shift their laying spots, and it's like Easter for a few days till I figure it out.

When a hen goes broody, she will sometimes do as my little Fayouma and disappear. Most of the time she'll just stop leaving one of the laying spots once the eggs are laid there. And at that point, I leave her alone.

Once or twice a day, a setting hen will leave the nest for a very short time- just long enough to get a drink of water, something to eat, and to use the Little Hen's Room. She will never leave the eggs long enough for them to cool off, though, so when I'm egg gathering and come across a hen-free nest with WARM eggs in it,

I leave them alone and just check back later to make sure she returns.

I've heard that chickens will sometimes break each other's eggs or kill each other's chicks. I've never had this happen and I think free ranging has a lot to do with this. There's not the territory stress related to being confined when you have the entire world as your hen house. Of course, my hens have the stress of living next to coyote-infested woods, but life is full of trade offs…

I have 2 pairs of hens who actually tag-team a nest. One pair consists of a Black Australorp and a Rhode Island Red, and the other pair is a Black Australorp and a Silky Bantam. They set right up against each other and take their breaks at different times. When the chicks hatch, they split them up pretty evenly to watch and raise up.

A word about Silky Bantams. They're hysterical looking. They appear hairy rather than feathered, they have feathers on their legs and a pincushionish topknot of feathers on their heads. They always seem confused, startled, annoyed, or an amazing combination of all three simultaneously. They are funny little chickens that lay funny little eggs.

As if that all weren't enough to justify a few running around the farm, they are the world's best setters of ANY eggs, not just their own or those of other chickens. I know of silkies that have hatched and raised ducklings, turkeys, and guinea hens.

Hens will lay an egg every day or so, but will not start setting till they deem their nest full enough. For some, that's two eggs. For others, over twenty. Rarely will all the eggs hatch from a very large nest- about half is all you should expect. So hatch day brings ALL the babies into the world at once. When everyone has been hatched and led off into the world, I'll don latex gloves and gingerly extract all the 'leftover' eggs. After three weeks of being kept warm, there will be a few 'real stinkers', and I've even had one explode as I placed it into the disposal sack, so be vewwwwwy vewwwwwy careful when you attempt this at home.

Once the chicklets have arrived, the only thing you have to do for them is make sure there is a water source low and shallow enough for the chicks to reach without drowning. Mama hen will teach them how and what to eat, where and when to sleep, and will protect them with every inch of her being till they are about 6-8 weeks old, when she'll proclaim them Grown Up, and move on to laying another clutch.

For the first few clutches hatched here on the farm, I'd follow them around and make sure mama hen saw me pour out some special baby chicken food (that awful looking gray stuff) for her babies. Finally, one hen watched me pour it out, gave me that one-eyed look of distain only a chicken can manage, and scratched up a huge juicy grub for her babies. With a final dismissive flick of her tail, she stalked away with her offspring in tow. Thereafter, I've only used the special baby chicken food (that awful looking gray stuff) for those replacement chickens who come to the farm through the

Next Easiest Way- The Incubator

There's really nothing hard about hatching chicks via incubation. If you can follow an average cooking recipe, you can run an incubator. The principles are the same- good ingredients, proper equipment, attention to directions, and the correct cooking temperature.

Incubators come in all shapes and sizes- from a tiny pod for 3 eggs, to a behemoth capable of hatching out hundreds at once. For the average family farm wishing to hatch out a few batches of eggs per year, the Styrofoam variety available at the local Tractor Supply or Farm and Fleet is more than sufficient. I've used the kind with a fan, and without, and can't really say I've noticed a difference in hatch rate. I turn the eggs by hand, not by automatic turner. I believe in the tenet that the less moving parts a thing has, the more difficult it is for me to break it.

Your ingredients, of course, are the eggs themselves. Clean (but not washed) eggs can be saved for up to a week at room temperature pointy end down in an egg carton. This should give you time to amass the embryos of your future flock. Once you have enough eggs, set up your incubator according to directions.

It should sit in a quiet place- somewhere it's not likely to be jostled, bumped, or subjected to strong drafts either hot or cold. Add water to the proper receptacles. Turn it on and give it overnight to make sure it's holding the proper temperature. The ideal temperature for chickens is right at 100F. Once the incubator is holding steady at 100F, it's time to add your eggs.

As you lay the eggs in the incubator, take a crayon and mark an 'X' on one side. Lay all the eggs X-up. You'll need to turn the eggs at least three times a day to keep the embryos from adhering to one side of the shell. Studies have shown that a hen will turn her eggs every HOUR, but clearly the hens don't have laundry, cooking, or outside employment to take up their spare time, so my eggs make do with the thrice daily routine. When turning the eggs, turn OVER the ends, not just flipping from side to side.

That's it. Make sure the temperature stays correct, the water doesn't dry up, and the pre-chickens get turned three times a day.

For 18 days.

The morning of the 19th day, fill ALL the water receptacles, remove both stoppers from the lid, and turn those babies one last time. From here on, all you do is peer through the windows and make sure the temperature stays at 100F- baby chicks make a lot of heat getting ready to hatch.

I love hatch day.

I hate hatch day.

Hatching is hard work, and it's supposed to be. Don't give in to the urge to 'help out'- it'll end up badly. Trust me.

Don't remove the chicks till they are fully dry, no matter how pitiful they sound and no matter how much they are rolling their unhatched siblings around the incubator- the movement and sound of the other chicks actually encourages those 'still inside' to get a wiggle on and get hatching.

My least stressful hatch day so far was this most recent. I actually timed incubation so that the last turning coincided with our leaving town for a few days- the only thing my pet sitter had to do was check the temperature.

On day 21 we arrived home mid-evening. I went straight to the incubator and lifted the lid to have 19 beautiful dry little chicks POUR over the sides. What a welcome home!

Newly hatched incubator chicks need to be treated the same as newly arrived hatchery chicks (since they're basically the same critter- without the airplane ride). Once dry, they need a warm, **Not Hot,** place to live. Unless you're hatching in the middle of winter (and why would you?), actual room temperature should be fine as long as there are no drafts. Our non- air-conditioned house stays right around 80 in the summertime, which is perfect for chicks. Heat lamps are WAY too hot for my peace of mind- they are a fire hazard and it's very easy to overheat chicks, which will kill them every bit as quickly as chilling. If there's a true need for auxiliary heat, please use a regular light bulb.

Make sure you dip each chick's beak into the water and have it watch you 'peck' at the food with your finger. Free feed them the Special Baby Chicken food (that awful looking gray stuff) and all the fresh water they want for the first week or so, then start adding scraps/scratch a little bit at a time.

Congratulations- you've just hatched out your very own next generation of poultry.

Acronyms to Live By
Or
WTSHTF and It's TEOTWAWKI Will You Be SOL Or LOL?

The Internet is a wonderful thing. Or a terrible thing. Depending on the user and the day, and the attitude of the user at any given moment of any given day.

Personally, I couldn't see what the Big Deal was back when my husband started making noise about getting a computer. My entire computer experience up to that point had to do with playing solitaire without shuffling, finding Carmen Sandiego, and doing general office stuff on an internal network.

For the first few months after the new refurbished computer came to reside at our house, I dusted it and looked on with bemusement as hubby hunted and pecked his way across the 'net. It was cute.

Then one day, he said "You know honey- we can get email now- wanna set up an email account?"

My horizons grew, and I began to spend time on the computer keeping in touch with people I used to have to actually TALK to on the phone.

I can't remember the exact moment I discovered Google, but I do know it was life changing and historic, mainly for my husband, who hasn't seen his computer since.

Before you feel TOO sorry for him,

a) He introduced me to the computer in the first place- if he had just continued his hunt/peck web surfing, my house would be clean, the yard would be tidy and this pile of laundry wouldn't be threatening to avalanche down on us- even I can only play so much solitaire, and after a while you cease to be concerned about Carmen Sandiego- she's a big girl, where she goes is really none of OUR business, and

b) I did take pity on him and purchase him a shiny new laptop computer one Christmas along with a wireless router. While I am sadly tied to one spot (at my desk in the comfiest room of the house, but STILL….) he can roam at will throughout our domicile and if he REALLY wanted to, could even surf the 'net from the Throne Room, if you get what I mean…

Along with learning the ropes of 'net surfing and the finer points of computer ownership and use (don't be deceived, I still can't tell a megazilch from a gigahurtz), I found I needed to learn a whole 'nuther language- Computer Acronym.

In the beginning it was confusing (is DH Dear Husband or Dancing Hamster?), and it seemed I was always waiting for others to BRB- from what I could gather, they were picking up their A's from the F after L-ing them O.

With the general (trend, downturn, spiral, tanking, apocalyptic cataclysm- the adjective will change according to the reporter) of the economy, more and more the acronyms WTSHTF and TEOTWAWKI are making their way out of the realms of the Furtively Glancing Tinfoil Hat Wearing in an Undisclosed Location (or FGTHWIAUL's) crowd and into the general Mom and Pop Just Trying to Do the Best We Can With What We Have (a.k.a. MAPJTTDTBWCWWWH's) 'net where I hang out. WTSHTF and TEOTWAWKI are usually accompanied by flashy advertisements for all that leftover Y2K stuff that (thankfully) was produced to never go bad.

So what to do about this universal Call to Prep? How much is hype, how much is true, how much is fanned by those REALLY needing to empty their warehouses of all the stockpiled cases of MRE's, and what is your gut feeling reaction to the happy knowledge that we won't have an answer till the reality is full upon us?

In general, Homesteaders are a thrifty lot.

We've learned to use, re-use, re-tool, re-work, re-pair and re-do every single item till it's gasping for breath and begs to just be re-cycled and be done already.

We don't pinch pennies, we suck them completely dry.

We've been saving for rainy days since we heard the story of The Flood in the church nursery, and are such experts that Noah could've done well to consult us while packing.

So the sudden Mainstream News about Living Green, Being Frugal, Self Sufficiency and Sustainability is not really News to us at all- it's our lifestyle.

Some of us who were around (and out of diapers) in the '70's remember similar calls to action back then. We remember the lines at the gas stations. We remember thinking "This will be good for us- life will get simpler, more ecologically friendly- surely America will see Its slothful greedy ways and turn from them, embracing Mother Nature and we'll float off into the sunset hand in hand in hand (insert "I'd Like to Teach the World to Sing" music here) with all our Brothers and Sisters. Please pass the brownies.

What really happened is that the above didn't.

This is not the place to point fingers and get all worked up about WHY it didn't.

We need to figure out what we are going to do about it NOW.

Not in a big ol' Global way, although that's important to care about, too.
But in a 'needing to care about and take care of those people you love who are right in this room with you' way.

Where you personally are in this scenario is important and going to sway your thinking.

The following tips are certainly not geared towards those who've been 'putting away and putting up' for years, and have carefully stored and cataloged supplies, plus the knowledge to go on once those supplies are depleted. I hold all ya'll in the highest regard, and could no more write about what you've done and are doing than I could write a builder's manual for a space station.

No, this is for the rest of us- those who's age, circumstances and/or scope of enlightenment have left us reading the current news, looking around and feeling decidedly nervous and unprepared.

This is also not going to touch on the pros and cons of a personal arsenal. Gun usage and ownership are intensely personal decisions and must be dealt with on an individual basis. Although it can be argued that a firearm or three are handy and necessary tools around the homestead in general, I know plenty of homesteaders who do not, and will not, have a firearm on their property.

Step One-
Remain calm.

Step Two-
Look at your current situation. If you were to become ill, say with a particularly nasty virus that kept you within yarking distance of your commode, would your family be out of breakfast food and laundry soap after 3 days? Start there. Do not let your pantry get down to dust bunnies and that last can of Vienna sausages. Begin with a week's worth of easily prepared, shelf stable (or frozen) food in the house at all times.

Step Three-
Pretend you are going camping for the weekend. Gather your items needed, right down to bug spray and matches (in a ziplock baggie). Check the batteries in the flashlight, toss in some spares and ziplock up 3 days' worth of non-perishable, ready to eat foodstuffs ***and a can opener***. Don't forget dish soap and a roll of TP. Get one

of those little wind-up radios. Toothbrushes, toothpaste, soap, deodorant. Plastic trash bags, a small hatchet, pocketknife and coil of rope. Now roll up a seasonally appropriate change of clothing for each family member into a large ziplock and stuff it all into a duffle bag (everything will fit- I promise you). Tuck as much money as you can spare (I've had as little as $20 and as much as $100) into one of the zipper pockets and stash the duffel in the trunk of your car along with a case of water and a few blankets if climate dictates.
Repeat for each vehicle in the family.
Congratulations- you've just assembled your BOB's (Bug Out Bags)
(And you thought this was gonna be hard)
The items packed should be tweaked according to your family, and certainly there are LOTS of other cool things that can be added, but the above items should be able to be had for under $100 per bag (not including the cash, silly), and those are the very basic basics.

Step Four-
Every time you go to the grocery store, buy a little extra of things your family will eat (no point in having 50 cans of fruit cocktail if everyone hates fruit cocktail). Staples like coffee, flour, baking mix, sugar, cocoa, coffee, rice, beans, oatmeal, coffee, plain pasta, salt, pepper, vanilla, coffee, can add up very quickly and stored properly, will store indefinitely. Don't forget paper products and cleaning products- and if you are space-challenged like most of us are, remember that things like dish detergent can be used for washing ANYTHING- laundry, children, pets. Likewise, items like honey and maple syrup can be used for sweeteners in lieu of sugar. When you buy over the counter medications, check the date and if they are 'long-dated' (over 3 years out), pick up an extra. Make sure you have lots of first aid stuff.

Step Five-
Learn to grow stuff.
Every little bit helps, and in fact makes meals healthier for both body and soul if there's even a bite in there that came out of YOUR garden, YOUR chickens, YOUR goats. Get a canner and

learn how to use it. If you are garden-challenged like I am, proceed to

Step Six-
Learn to wildcraft. Get books and go to classes that teach you what weeds are edible- you'll be amazed by the variety out there in even the lowliest urban vacant lot (just be sure it hasn't been poisoned and even then wash it REALLY well…….ewwwww)

Step Seven-
Think beyond the Grid.
Your family is not doomed just because your bank account does not contain $10,000 for an off-grid power supply. Again- think 'camping'. Imagine the electric is turned off for a week- how ELSE can you heat, cool, draw water, cook, do laundry, see in the dark? Low tech Rocks. Have at least a few oil lanterns and spare oil and wicks. Make sure you have wood put up for cooking/heating (if you don't have a woodstove- even a little one, make that a priority- if you live where you CAN'T have a woodstove, have a grill- even a little hibachi one, and a good supply of charcoal). Where do you get your water? Where COULD you get your water? What would you need to do to make it potable? A gallon of bleach (unscented) goes a long, long way. Get a washboard, washtub and wringer. When your friends comment on the new Folksy decorating touches in your house, just smile and change the subject.
Here's where SMALL livestock comes in very handy. If I don't have a refrigerator/freezer or a small army to feed, I don't need a steer or pig. I need chickens and goats beCAUSE chickens and goats will keep my eggs, milk and meat fresh for me till I can use them in handy serving sizes.

Step Eight-
Never stop learning.
It matters not if you have 5 years' worth of food stocked up, if your SHTF for 6 years, you will still be SOL. Once your sugar is gone, what is out there that you can learn to grow/gather that will REPLACE sugar? And so on and so on.

And maybe nothing bad WILL happen.
Maybe our economy will turn around overnight due to the sudden overwhelming influx of money from the many new jobs created by the New Green Sustainable World, and we'll all float off into the sunset holding hands with our Brothers and Sisters, singing songs and eating brownies. That would be swell.

But here's the thing.

There doesn't HAVE to be a large noisy messy Event.

Because the truth of the matter is that every minute of every day in every neighborhood in every city EVERYWHERE, the S is HTF for someone, somewhere. And it signals TEOTWA(they)KI.

A father is laid off. A wife is diagnosed with a medical condition. A child is in an accident. There's drought, flooding, tornadoes, hurricanes, ice, heat, SOMETHING that takes everything a family has worked so hard for and makes it…gone.

The funny thing about fear is that it either renders a body paralyzed, or makes it capable of vaulting through fire and into bravery.

If a family is faced with loss and has never considered loss before, it's easily paralyzed.
But if that same family has considered loss (calmly), and made a conscious effort to gain the knowledge to feed itself, care for itself, and go on from wherever fate lands it, even if the larder is NOT stocked for years, that knowledge will be invaluable.

Knowledge is power.

Power is liberating.

Liberty is sweet.

In the movie Ice Age, the mammoth, the sloth and the tiger are trying to get food for the human baby they are caring for. They come across a HUGE flock of dodo birds who seem irrationally protective of a few watermelons. The conversation goes generally like this-

Dodo- "This is our private stockpile for the Ice Age. Sub-arctic temperatures will force us underground for a billion billion years."

Mammoth- "So you got three melons?"

Dodo- "If YOU weren't smart enough to plan ahead, then DOOM ON YOU."

It's good for a great belly laugh, cuz obviously, three melons were not going to sustain a whole flock of birds for a billion billion years.
Or would they?

What if the dodos had PLANTED those watermelon seeds in their underground caverns warmed and lit by the volcano and watered by snow?

And clearly, the mammoth, the sloth and the tiger had no place mocking the dodos; since three melons were exactly three more melons then THEY had come up with.

I really think the dodos would have come out all right if their last female hadn't launched herself off that cliff…

My 8-year-old son is concerned about 2012. The End of the World (literally the End of the Age) in the Mayan calendar.
I've gotta admit that it creeped me out more than a little bit too.
Until it occurred to me.
Why can't the New Age be ultimately a Better Age?

Without a doubt, the end of the Oil Age will be a bad thing for a lot of people and a lot of our society's infrastructure. But aren't we as homesteaders already ON that path to the New Age?

Think out of the box.

Do what you can, as you can do it.

Love your family. Enjoy life.

Remain calm.

Don't Quit Your Day Job Bringing Home the Bacon So You Can Afford to Feed the Pigs

Dreaming about living in the country is easy, even when you're not quite there.

Rural images ripple unbidden through burbling brooks of the mind like so many flashing, darting minnows- abrupt, startling sensory overlays to whatever is passing for reality at the time.

Steaming in stalled traffic, toxic fumes rising from the tailpipes of a million other commuters, all windows closed to the stench, breathing 'conditioned' air, radio turned full up to stifle the cacophony of a million other radios and a million other engines, right in the middle of a nice mental image of ramming your car into the one ahead of you, and the one ahead of THAT one, and the one ahead of THAT one, (poof) and you're in the middle of a field of cows- nice clean cows with doe like eyes and lashes to die for, all contentedly chewing on their organic cuds. Perhaps humming something classical under their chlorophyll-scented breath. Inhale. Exhale. Repeat.

Cubicle, inbox, outbox, sticky pads, telephone, rolling black chair (kept carefully on the hard plastic carpet guard), office gossip circulates, virus-like, infecting everyone it touches. There must be no softness shown, no sympathy, no common sense, and above all no refusal to pick a side. You MUST be on a side, you must choose, this is important to the well-being of the entire universe, this ISSUE must be cussed, discussed, discovered, covered, recovered, hashed, rehashed, solved, resolved, until it's unrecognizable from whatever it started out to be (were we deciding between plain/coated paper clips, or pizza/salads for lunch???). There's an opening, a tiny imperceptible rift in the space between gray fabric covered co-workers and gray fabric covered cubicle wall and a break is made- to the ladies' room! The door slams shut, the latch is latched and the body slumps onto the stool- head spinning, breathing in the carefully sterilized aroma of

Lysol, glass cleaner and as many different perfumes as there are women in the office. Torn as to the next logical action- laughter, screaming, head banging or just giving up and flushing yourself, (poof) and you're in a vegetable garden. Sun shining, the earth warm and fragrant under your bare feet, the tomatoes could be harvested blindfolded; they're so intoxicatingly spicy. Inhale. Exhale. Repeat.

(Only one more, I promise…)

Arriving home after a day at work, the odor of cooking wafts through the air. Someone else's cooking. In someone else's apartment. The sound of someone else's child pounding on something while singing off key at the top of their tiny voice can be heard over the chorus of a herd of television sets all marching to the tune of different drummers. Wearily, drapes closed to the mirror images of your life across the street, you pet the cat in your lap and (poof) you and the cat are sitting in a rocking chair in front of a fireplace. The pitter-patter of raindrops on the roof keeps time with the spring peepers' concert literally over the river and through the woods. There's a pie in the oven. Apple pie. Made with apples from your apple tree. Inhale. Exhale. Repeat.

If only. If only there was a way to get from here to there…the dream becomes a mission and the mission becomes an obsession and the obsession becomes (poof) a place in the country with your name on the mortgage. Inhale. Exhale. Hyperventilate.

Suddenly all the above becomes reality. But what you didn't think about is that most likely ALL the above becomes reality. The good, the bad, the urban, the rural, the paper clips and the tomatoes. A big ol' simultaneous mess of clashing lifestyles that it becomes horrifyingly clear is YOUR new lifestyle, because you need that hated job to pay for that loved homestead. Inhale. Turn blue. Pass out.

Some folks have the sense to save up for a country place during their working years, retire with a nice party and a gold watch, pack up the U-Haul and move into a paid for dwelling nestled on acreage. Once a month, their retirement check is deposited in their account and they pay their bills. Easy.

Some folks have the good fortune to be born on a large family farm where it's assumed that home is already here, and you are already home.

Some folks have a pre-learned trade, skill, knowledge or some such that allows them to actually make a living without ever leaving the property.

Then there are the rest of us.

Oh, I know the bookshelves at Amazon are chock full of tomes preaching that if a soul is serious about being a True Homesteader, everything that's needed will be produced by the sweat of your brow and spring from the loins of your property, but I'm here to witness honestly that I've been at this Small Homesteader Thing for well nigh a quarter of a century and I've yet to be able to pay all my farm bills from something I do that's actually farm-related.

I do have a Homestead. And I'm right proud and serious about it. But while I've always managed to raise up, sell, plant, harvest and otherwise oversee creation of things that bring in some cash to defray the cost of the farm proper, I've always had to have employment off the farm to pay for those little luxuries like clothing for the children, upkeep on vehicles, health/auto/property insurance, taxes, and stuff we can't grow, like toilet paper and ink pens.

I've tried to work a normal job during normal hours and still maintain the farm, and it's a dreary, precarious slog. When my co-workers were enjoying a cuppa and the morning paper before their drive in to work, I'd been up already for at least an hour, milking goats, tending horses, and then diving into the shower to become halfway presentable, and most always not quite making it- the stray hay in my coat pocket, forgetting to take off my 'barn shoes' before leaving for work, arriving to work just a tad late because I forgot to turn off the water hose to the horse tanks and had to turn around and go home to turn it off- all proof to the world that you can take this old gal physically off of the farm, but it always follows me like a fed cat.

Daylight savings time is a particularly nasty season for normally employed small homesteaders. For fully half the year the critters get fed in the dark in the morning, and fed in the dark at night. It's almost enough to make anyone throw in the towel and move on back into town.

But here's the thing. Just because you need a 'real' job to support your country living dreams, doesn't mean you're stuck in the 9 to 5/M-F nightmare.

The first thing that needs to be addressed is that 9 to 5/M-F is an inconvenient time to be away from the farm. That's daylight. And when the Vet is available. And….daylight. So the first logical option is that if there are multiple shifts at your workplace, apply for your same position, but not 1st shift. Either 2nd or 3rd shifts are good options for homesteaders. (And they generally pay more, which is an extra bonus).

Are you trained in something that's open to working flextime? Many medical positions can be arranged so that you can work say, 3 twelve hour shifts instead of 5 eights. I know one Flight for Life nurse who works 2 sixteen-hour shifts and is done for the week. If there's no Dr. in front of your name, and no RN or LVN behind it, there's a wide assortment of 2-year degrees that would afford the same schedules- X-ray tech, lab tech- check out your local community college for the different courses. While the thought of having to go back to school for 2 years may give you the heebie jeebies, stop and think a minute about being trapped in your cubicle for another 20 years. Better?

Do you have small children? Do you LIKE to have children around? Daycare is a wide open field, and depending on where your farm is located, there may be a niche waiting for small people to enjoy YOUR wide open fields while their moms work at the jobs you don't want to, and pay you to stay on your homestead,

Bless their hearts. Make sure to check state and local guidelines regarding certification and insurance requirements.

Keep your eyes and ears open at your current employment- when there was a brand new position coming up at my workplace, I was offered the job and I took it even though my original intent was to QUIT as soon as I could afford it. The benefit of being the first person on a job is that there's no existing job description, and the possibility of writing your own and pretty much making up the job as you go is both an awesome responsibility and wonderfully freeing. While I won't even pretend that if we won the lottery tomorrow I'd stay on my job for the love of it, it's been just what we've needed to allow us to do what we need to do on the farm, and for our family. Of course I'm very careful not to take advantage of that freedom.

An online home computer is a rural person's friend. Whether you're looking up the dosage of penicillin to give a feverish goat, finding planting tips for State Fair-worthy eggplants, or finding employment, the answers are truly right there in front of us. Everyone knows SOMEONE who works from home with the help of his or her computer. The work may be repetitive and mind numbingly boring, but if you can put in your hours and get the work done, some character on your farm will be happy to liven things up a bit for you- there are fences to jump over or get hung up in, other characters to be fought with, courted inappropriately, or eaten, and general mayhem waiting to occur at any given moment. It continually amazes me that my animal family is so devoted to making sure that I'm never bored, and it's brought a tear to my eye more than once. Really.

Obviously, anything promising many dollars for little work should be researched with extreme caution, or avoided altogether.

While most folks have a goal of making their farm a Working Venture, the truth is that it takes time, trial and error and money to achieve this in any way, form or manner.

Can you eventually make your living from dairy goats, fiber animals, free-range hens, grass fed beef and organic produce? Yes. No. Maybe. The hard fact is that there's a learning curve to all the above, and all the above need to be approached in a tiny way at first- these are living things who will depend on you for everything they have including the quality of their very lives, even the plants.

And even IF there is a ready market for piebald miniature llamas in your area this year, there may not be next year. But I'll bet dollars to donuts that your own operating expenses will still be there, up to and including X number of sacks of Llama Chow every week.

Be very, very sure of your consumer base.

Start small, no matter how excited you are to start.

Grow slowly, no matter how excited you are to grow.

And always, always have a Plan B for the rainy day when the bottom falls out and pulls out the rug under your feet with it.

Having to have a 'real job' does not mean you are a failure at Homesteading. All it means is that right now, at this moment, your goal of a successful homestead requires this of you. It's to your credit that your homestead means enough for you to do what you need to do to attain and maintain it.

The only real failure is not to try at all.

The silver lining of having to work off the farm is that while you are stuck in traffic or your cubicle, when you get (poofed) to that idyllic scenario in your head, it's not just a dream- if you can keep from throttling the copy machine, your co-workers or disgruntled customers for just a few more hours, you WILL be sitting in your rocking chair with your cat in your lap, listening to the rain pitter patter on the roof. Inhale. Exhale. Repeat. Smile.

Homeschooling for Homesteaders
The One Room Schoolhouse is Alive and Well

As modern day homesteaders, we believe from our heads to our hearts that we MUST reject a lot of what is taken for granted by the rest of our society. Not just on a whim, or a curious fluke in our personalities, but by the very real knowledge that our modern society is not well in many ways, and if we continue to immerse ourselves and our families in it, we will soon be ailing right along with it.

So we make the move from the city to the country, limit (or eliminate) electronic mind-killers like the TV and the Playstation, and boot those young'ns outside to run wild and free without the fear of traffic, or kidnappers, or drive by shootings.

They rise early in the morning to the sound of the rooster, the smell of the earth, and a breakfast of natural whole foods.

And then, they go... where?

If your children are between the ages of 5 and 16, they go to school, of course.

Here in the U.S. of A., we have a ginormous monstrosity called the Public School System. It's a wonderful idea in theory, and the reality of it is that MOST of the time, in MOST of the places, it works reasonably well.

But, just like everything else, we as parents must do OUR homework regarding our local school(s), for, beCAUSE our country is so big and so diverse, and beCAUSE by the very nature of "federal control" things that are supposed to be standardized in a good way generally get standardized in a mediocre way, whether your family's assigned public school is going to be a great one, an acceptable one, a miserable one, or an outright dangerous one is very much a crap shoot.

And here's the funny part (if you are a fan of dark humor): WHERE the school is located does NOT dictate what your children's experience will be. There are many, many inner city schools populated by teachers and parents whose dedication to their children is amazing, and many, many schools in affluent communities whose children are routinely dying of drug overdoses while their parents are chasing the next monetary goal. The majority of public schools, like the majority of the rest of life, fall somewhere in that huge grey middle area.

Chapter One - Our Public School Experience

Oddly enough (for a home-schooler), I've had good public school experiences, both personally and with my children's education.

I attended public schools back in the day of small classes, teachers who commonly came to dinner at the homes of the students, room-mothers there almost daily to help with projects, and the ability to go to the bathroom without needing a key to get into it. Oh yeah, and there was no such thing as metal detectors at the front door, or school security. Every door into the school was unlocked, all day every day. Up until my older boy was in high school, this remained generally unchanged - even in the dark days of the mid 70's race problems in high schools, there was no lock down, and if you moved in an already mixed group (like I did), there was no fear - only a sad confusion at the rest of the mess, but we felt that most of the time anyway.

My daughter tested into our local public school system's Gifted and Talented Program. By that time we had moved out to the country, but were still within the urban school system. The Gifted and Talented Program had been set up in, unarguably, the most inner of the inner-city schools, in a city of over 80,000 souls. They had set up the program so that 50% of the students were those who tested into it, and 50% were neighborhood children whose parents chose to have them attend their neighborhood school, rather than be bussed out of the neighborhood to the nearest "normal" school.

My 5-year-old's bus ride every morning exceeded 45 minutes, and took her all over the area to pick up the other Lighthouse students, but because of where we were living, it would have taken her that long to get to the nearest "local" school anyway, with the bus stopping at every corner and farm.

Although my (then) husband was EXTREMELY skeptical of the wisdom behind bussing our child INTO the very city we worked so hard to get OUT of, and yea, verily, straight into the heart of the worst part of it, plus his concern that the lessons would have to be "dumbed down" to accommodate the "local" children, I felt that we needed to give it a try and see what happened.

What happened was remarkable.

Of course, our own child blossomed in an environment that was geared towards individual thought and learning. She's a genius.

The remarkable part (at least to my husband), was watching what happened to the neighborhood kids - none of whom had tested into the Gifted and Talented Program via the pre-kindergarten testing process.

They not only blossomed, they were an explosive riot of veritable flowers.

When it was just assumed that ALL the children would be not only capable, but would thrive under the Gifted and Talented Instruction, without exception, they were, and did.

My daughter's experience in the Lighthouse Program taught her at a very early age that people come in all shapes, sizes, colors and backgrounds, and that it is a mistake to label anyone according to what is visible on their outsides.

My older son attended our "local" public school (although he's also clearly a genius, little 5-year-old boys tend not to sit still and test as well as little 5-year-old girls). This school was brand new, built to service not only the rural families in the area, but all the new subdivisions sprouting up in what used to be fields like so many noxious weeds. Although the education he received was a good one (this school was touted as one of Wisconsin's finest grade schools), the lack of social diversity in the students clearly colored his views (literally) - and as a young adult he still exhibits some vestiges of that.

Although I'm aware that little boys tend to emulate their fathers and little girls tend to emulate their mothers, and there's a very real difference in the way this particular set of parents viewed the world and the people in it, I'm convinced that being exposed only to little children of like backgrounds for his entire early-schooling years didn't help.

Both of these children grew up healthy and literate and have gone on to successful college careers and (in the case of the elder one) successful professional careers, thereby proving that a lot of the time, public school works.

WHERE THE HECK IS THE STUFF ABOUT HOME-SCHOOLING????

Enter child number three, born to a different (half of it anyway) set of parents, in a different state, and at a different time of life for these parents.

This child was born at home, with a midwife, in a 100-plus-year-old house at the edge of a tiny town in Texas. I had a part time job, meaning that Alec had to go to daycare several days a week and we found a wonderful one run by a wonderful woman - home cooked meals, lots of outside playtime, lots of hands on activities rather than sit-still-and-listen activities. Delia has an after-school-pickup section of her daycare, and in the spring before her little charges turn kindergarten age, they take a field trip to the school to get them familiar with where they will be going in the fall.

We had already toyed with the idea of home-schooling since, by this time, my employment offered me the freedom to take my child with me to work if I wanted to, and with him being all of almost five, he could be taken without CONSTANT supervision, allowing me to actually, you know, WORK at work.

We went on the field trip to the school. Out of 12 families, only 2 parents attended, and I thought it was odd that I was one of them, since we were thinking of NOT enrolling our child in this school. One would think that one would be interested in checking out one's child's school... Our local school is considered very good; it gets wonderful ratings by the Texas Education Association, and indeed, when we walked through the front doors, we were met with a cacophony of colors and sounds all touting the Fun of Learning, and our son was clearly psyched about it. Hyperactively so. His excitement was contagious, and I was tempted to be swept into it all along with him...

Until....

I looked up and saw The Banner.

Over the entry to the main corridor was a banner proclaiming this school one of Texas' Finest, signed (supposedly) by the President of the United States of America, and boldly (even aggressively) stating:

NO CHILD LEFT BEHIND

I know that this phrase is supposed to be uplifting, comforting and encouraging, and in my former, younger, newer life as a parent, it probably would have been.

Since I am twenty years older, have been around life's block a few times, and have now seen our government and society at work, it struck me like a slap across the face as being creepy and menacing.

And I knew at that moment, for sure and for certain, that THIS child would NOT be attending public school.

Chapter Two - The "Why" of Home-schooling

Each family has their own personal reasons to home-school, but whether those reasons are religious, political, or having to do with the child's needs not being met by the public school system, the gist of the matter is basically the same as why we homestead - we want to KNOW what's going into our children's heads is as pure and true as what we are so careful to put into their tummies and their lungs.

I feel compelled to add here that my initial thoughts about home schooling were completely and absolutely self-serving. Ward goes to work at 8:30 AM. I go to work after lunch. The local school starts promptly (a word I have trouble with on the BEST of days) at 7:45 AM. I had a difficult time justifying hauling our 5-year-old to "work" well before the adults in the family had to be at theirs. Then, on the other end of it, Ward and I both get out of work at 6:00 PM - well AFTER the school lets out at 2:45. Of course there's Delia's after-school care, but for a young child to spend eleven hours out of every day in the care of adults who are not their parents seems more than a little unnatural to us.

I understand and sympathize with parents who have no other choice than the above scenario - I spent several years as a single working mother myself. We do the best we can with the options at our disposal. Depending on your employment, sometimes home-schooling can still be accomplished - if you are able to work "odd" shifts, child care can sometimes be arranged for when you are working, and you will be with your child(ren) during the day to school them.

The fact that a large part of our society considers it normal and healthy to deposit their young into the care of "others" for a huge part of their waking hours, *and* from the time they are 6 weeks old, is, to our way of thinking, certainly a sign of the not-wellness of our culture.

At the present time, we are fortunate enough to have the freedom to both home-school AND be gainfully employed, so we started looking at the all-children-should-go-to-public-school idea very closely.

And just like a platypus, the more closely we looked at public school, the odder it started looking.

Figures provided by the schools themselves admit that a mere 2 hours is spent in actual school-learnin' for the average elementary-schooler each day. The rest of the 8 hours or so is spent taking turns, waiting in line, recess, lunch, bathroom breaks, etc.

I called our local school to find out the average class size for kindergarten.

Thirty.

They have thirty 5-year-olds vs. ONE teacher.

I asked how many teachers' aides were in each class and was laughed at.

I asked if they took advantage of room-mothers to come in and provide extra hands, eyes and hearts to this mass of young humanity and was told, "that's NOT allowed."

Wait a minute....

"NOT ALLOWED"???? *I'M* not allowed into my own child's classroom during the day???

Apparently not.

Home school was looking better and better.

In fairness, the next school system over has a kindergartener-teacher ratio of 15-1, which would have been perfectly acceptable to me.

Then there's the question of homework. Our neighbor's boy is the same age as ours. He spends all day in public school and comes home with at least an hour's worth of homework. In SECOND GRADE. What in the world is there for a second-grader to learn that cannot be accomplished in 8 hours at school???

One of my best friends is an elementary school principal, and she was a teacher for years and years before that. She was understandably skeptical about our interest in home schooling (since she's known me for almost 30 years, I'm sure she saw right past all my "for public consumption" reasons and saw my inherent slothfulness shining through). From watching Cathy over the years, I know that the majority of teachers teach because they love their students. I know that they spend literally thousands of their own dollars purchasing materials for their kids to make up for the shortcomings of the materials they are given with which to teach. I know that they are frustrated by the fact that they must take a large portion of every school-year "teaching to the test" - preparing their students for the standardized testing that will determine what their schools receive in the way of funding.

Our final analysis of public schools is that the public school system is aimed at educating the Average Student. Anyone who's known even one child knows that not a single one is average; all are uniquely gifted and learn at different rates and in different ways.

To take all the knowledge that needs to be learned by all the children in the country and force it into a single mold is like asking a federal committee to construct a duck.

You get a platypus.

While agreeing with me in concept, Cathy challenged me, asking exactly HOW I was planning on carrying out something as important as my child's education all by my lonesome, without any formal training.

It was an excellent question.

Chapter Three - The "How" of Home-schooling

There are as many ways to home-school as there are home-schooling families. And this is as it should be, because that's the whole point. If you want your child to have an education exactly like he/she'd get in public school, you'll save a whole lot of time and money if you just enroll him/her and be done with it. As stated before, they will most likely turn out just fine.

There are several general types of teaching styles used to home-school and I'll briefly touch on each one. A wise parent will change the style of teaching depending on the individual child's needs. I know some home-schooling families who have all the styles going on at once with different children, and some who even have some in public school and some out - the main issue is not To Home-school or

Not to Home-school, the main issue at all times should be, “Where/how will my child learn and grow the best at this particular time?”

Traditional home-schoolers have School at Home. There is usually a designated school area or room that’s set up with desks or study areas for each child. Lessons are taught basically the same as in "regular" schools.

Child Directed Learning is a little trickier. Using this style, the parent takes what the child is already interested in and turns it into school. Dinosaurs? This of course encompasses Science, but also history, reading, math (dino story problems, reading really, really big numbers BC), and art. Whole units are done up this way, and the materials you were going to teach anyway are cleverly disguised as your child's own ideas.

There are many "boxed" curriculums designed in the above two styles. When we started our home-schooling adventure, we chose a curriculum that is modified Child Directed - there are pretty basic reading, math and language presentations, along with a lot of emphasis on music, science and art. One thing I really like about it is that it’s set up in weekly lessons rather than daily lessons, giving me the freedom to type up my daily schedule according to my own work needs for the week - some days we will do more school than others. I keep the typed schedules along with his finished workbooks for future reference as proof that we really are teaching him stuff.

As we've gotten more comfortable with teaching, we've picked up books to add to our curriculum - science books, history books, poetry books, books on spiritualism. We have lessons on our old upright piano. We purchased and very much like Rosetta Stone Spanish. With only one student, I can teach everything required from the curriculum AND our added materials in 4 mornings per week.

There are three 12 week quarters to the printed work, so we school September-November and take all of December off, school January-March and take all of April off, and school May-July and take all of August off. One of the many perks of this particular curriculum is that any time after the 4th grade, we may choose to go online with our schooling - he'll be assigned a teacher who will be available to grade projects, give help and provide transcripts. If he chooses to home-school through high school, he will receive an accredited diploma, and will be paired with a counselor in his senior year who will help him fill out college applications (if that's where he wants to go), navigate through the SAT's and apply for scholarships. I'm a fan of all this extra help, since I'm pretty sure he'll surpass me intellectually somewhere in the next 5 years.

Un-schoolers' style is to not have a style... Life Is School. This is generally too scary a concept for most new home-schoolers because you really need to take a Big Picture view of schooling, and make really good notes of everything you do during the course of each day, then review at the end of the week/month/year to make sure you've introduced everything that was age-appropriate. Cooking together= Fractions and Chemistry. Grocery shopping = Budgeting and Math. Planting a garden = Biology and PhysEd.

Again, there are multitudinous variations of all of the above, including scary mutations on either end - the parent whose goal is to have their child enrolled in Harvard by the age of 12 and who pretty much spends that child's childhood turning them into a miniature adult; the parent who is home-schooling to keep their child protected from the Evils of the

World and whose child is terrified of anyone who smiles at them and says hello in the grocery store; the parent who believes that the child will learn what he/she needs to know just by living and sets no boundaries, no limits, gives no direction.... all crazy scary.

Chapter Four- What about Socialization???

This is the Battle Cry of the Public Schoolers. How, they ask, will a home-schooled child learn to get along with others? To share? To behave in society?

Let's look at this a moment.

In public school, children are segregated according to age. They spend all day in the company of their peers, and maybe a year or two older or younger during recess and lunchtime. And recess and lunchtime are the only times they will have for free play and interaction all day long. The rest of the time is spent sitting still and being quiet.

When else in all of life does this occur? In your own personal workplace, are workers separated by age? At church, in our neighborhoods, ANYWHERE else in society???

I'm not saying that the answer is to keep your home-schooled children to themselves - far from it.

I am lucky enough to be a member of a small, close-knit home-school group. By lucky, I don't mean that I was lucky enough to find ***A*** home-school group, there are many groups out there in which to belong. By lucky, I mean that this particular group is wildly diverse. We have members who are home-schooling for all the reasons listed above, and here's the cool part - it doesn't matter to any of us WHY we are home-schooling - we are there to support each other.

Although most of our members are Christians, some attend huge urban churches, some tiny rural family churches. We have members who have children who are autistic and/or who have attention deficit disorder and would be put in the "special ed" classes at public school - these are not mentally challenged kids, mind you, they merely think differently and need to be taught in non-mainstream ways.

I am the token quasi-heathen-reincarnationist-Old-Hippiechick, and I am embraced along with everyone else. We have members with "blended" families, members who have bi-racial families. I love our group.

In any given week there will be a number of activities to partake of: field trips, classes, community service projects, 4-H group, soccer league.

My son recently had his birthday party and I was struck yet again that it WAS simpler to have birthday parties for my public school kids - in school you know all kids in your class. Period. You don't know their siblings or other family members. As home-schoolers we know entire families. My eight-year-old son had children at his party from the age of 4 months to 12 years, girls and boys, moms and dads.

It was marvelous - not a gang of same aged boys, but a huge extended family gathering.

My son can go anywhere, relate and talk to anyone, of any age, anywhere. He can go to a real restaurant, read a menu, order for himself and behave. He can go on a museum tour and ask intelligent questions. To me, this IS socialized -

being comfortable and able to conduct himself in any segment of society at any given time and place.

We are so enjoying home-schooling, and it's really been ideal for us in another way: my husband has faced some serious health challenges that have forced us to be away from home, more than not, for the last 9 months. Instead of worrying about how we will split up the family (do I leave our son with friends who will get him to school, or leave my husband alone in a hospital 5 hours from home?), we pack up the schoolwork with our clothes, and hit the museums and sights in the Big City.

If at some point, our son expresses interest in enrolling in public school, and as long as our public school remains as safe and secure as a public school can be, off he'll go - with the understanding that once enrolled, it's a commitment, and he must stay in school at least till the end of that school year. Again, the bottom line is encouraging the child to grow into a responsible adult and learn at his/her own pace, in his/her own manner.

The very essence of home-schooling is that we keep our children out of public school not because they will learn too MUCH about life and the world there, but because a school building cannot possibly contain all the wonders of life and the world - for that must be gotten on the fly, in the fields, museums, parks, caves, theaters, restaurants, festivals and planetariums. From the tiny organisms in the earth beneath our feet to as far as the eye can see, to Infinity and Beyond.

If my child grows up realizing that what he learns in "school" is not the sum of what he needs to know, but the foundation to learn all there is to discover....

I will have succeeded as a parent, and a teacher.

Barn Cats- Thugs of the Homestead

Working when they feel like it, sleeping the day away, partying all night, and making sure you know that whatever you say or do means not a whit to them (what IS a whit, anyway?), these creatures who inhabit a homestead do not hop, trot, gallop, waddle or run like the other resident critters- they saunter.

Saunter around the corner just in time for dinner.

Saunter away with a mouse after a lightning quick hunt ends successfully.

Saunter purposefully after doing something embarrassing, exuding "I meant to do that" from every furry pore.

Saunter right in front of your legs while you are carting in 50-pound bags of feed, or better yet- groceries. The sack with the breakables in it.

The fuzzy equivalent to the relation who comes to visit, and then stays long past his welcome, not with appreciation, but with the attitude that he's doing you a big fat hairy favor by consuming YOUR food and using YOUR utilities, you know of course who I'm talking about.

The barn cat.

Why on earth would we keep a creature around that seems to be in permanent teenaged morosity? "To catch the mice," we claim defiantly.

Really.

Really?

I currently have three cats in residence.

Gremlin was born here 12 years ago. His mom was a tiny feral fluff of a kitty who had 2 kittens under the house. Shortly after the kitties were weaned, momma cat disappeared with the cute kitten, and Gremlin was left. Mostly wild, he's prime Farm Cat material, yet if confronted, nay, presented with a mouse, he turns his back and yawns. I've witnessed him hastily pulling his paw away from danger of coming in contact with a running mouse.

Petri was a friend's cat. When Angela moved out of state, Petri came to live with us. Angela had found Petri as a starving stray kitten, and bottle-fed him into a sleek, panther-like specimen. He had been denied transfer due to a fondness of urinating on everything inside the house, so even though he had had his front claws removed, he was dubbed a Barn Cat, and turned loose. I've seen him catch one mouse in 8 years. It was slow, and looked a little brain-damaged. Petri is a prime example of 'you are, what you eat'.

Oswald was born in the lap of luxury- the planned child of two housecats. Fluffy, orange and white, with whiskers all the way out to there, Oswald lived in our house till we started the big noisy alarming parts of our home renovation, at which point he showed his displeasure by using our bed as a litter box. After a few such episodes, I picked up the cat, opened the front door, and unceremoniously plopped him onto the porch, closing the door behind me.

Guess he showed ME.

Surprisingly, Oswald is the Master Mouser- he can hear a mouse from across the yard and through an insulated wall. If I come across a mouse in a feed sack, all I have to do is say 'here Ozzie' and he's right there to retrieve it for me. I tip the sack and in he darts, backing out with the offending rodent. If there are TWO mice in the sack, that's his specialty- it only takes a split second longer, then he backs out with a mouse-tashe, one tail drooping out of each side of his mouth.

For the squeamish mouse lovers out there- Ozzie is also the most businesslike cat I've ever seen. He's not interested in the least with playing with his hapless prey. It's a quick execution, followed by happy ingestion.

Here's where the informational part of this story begins…

There are many myths surrounding the amount of care and upkeep needed by the average barn cat, and perhaps the most harmful one is

If you do not feed your barn cats, they will be better hunters

The truth is, if you do not feed your barn cats, they will get very skinny and leave. Or die. Or both. Cats hunt for one reason only- the personal satisfaction and pleasure they receive from causing something smaller than them to be very afraid, and then killing it. Well-fed barn cats will be stronger, happier, and quicker.

Won't it cost a lot to feed a lot of cats? Of course it will. Therefore, I recommend not HAVING a lot of cats, which is caused by another myth

Barn cats are a renewable resource

There is not much cuter than a litter of kittens. If you have an unspayed female cat, you will soon know the joy of frolicking kittens. Cats reproduce at an amazing rate of speed. A female cat will be ready to breed any time after about 5 months of age. At this time they come into season, which is accompanied by caterwauling and a (to tomcats) very seductive way of locomotion that looks to the casual observer like they've been hit by a fast-moving vehicle causing the fracture of several vertebrae. This attractive behavior will continue till they are spayed, or impregnated.

Left to their own devices, a female cat will have two litters of kitties per year. The average litter is 4 kittens. If half of them are female, you will have 8 frolicking kittens the first year. Twenty boisterous kittens the second year. One hundred and twenty truly horrifying kittens the third year. And by the fourth year, you will have to move to a new place, because the SIX HUNDRED KITTENS will make your current place a complete wasteland.

Make some calls. Your local shelter should be able to direct you to low cost spay/neuter clinics or programs that will sterilize your cats and give them a rabies shot for a nominal fee. Sure, it costs money, but nothing like trying to keep SIX HUNDRED KITTENS in food.

Of course, it's highly unlikely that you will actually be facing SIX HUNDRED KITTENS. Your neighbors may take a few. Your friends and family may take a few. An ad in the Thrifty Nickel may snag homes for a few. If you are really out in the boondocks, hawks (or gators) may even take a few. And you may be sure, if you do not vaccinate your cats, disease will take more than a few, proving wrong the myth that

Barn cats do not need to be vaccinated

Of course they do.

In fact, it is required by law that they are up to date on rabies vaccinations, which, depending on your state is either given annually or every three years.

Additionally, cats (especially outside cats or large groups of cats) are very susceptible to some other unpleasant and potentially fatal diseases. Feline Distemper is very contagious, and even though it's rarely fatal (unlike Canine Distemper), it's still a drag to be surrounded by a bunch of cats with snotty noses and runny eyes. You can vaccinate against this, Calicivirus and herpes virus, in a combo vaccine known as the FRP. These are considered "core" vaccines, and are essential for all cats. A 4-way vaccine, adding Chlamydia is also available, and for the extra few cents, a really good idea, even though the chance of a human catching Chlamydia from a cat is extremely unlikely. Feline Leukemia is a good vaccination to consider- if contracted, a cat can either be a carrier who can pass it on to other cats, or break with it themselves- and it's always fatal.

Lastly, and dependant on the tameness of your cats and the intestinal fortitude of yourself and your helpers (never attempt doctoring a cat by yourself), cats should be periodically wormed, and treated for fleas and/or ear mites. Make sure any treatments you are giving only need to be given once a month, maximum. Cats remember. And act/react accordingly. Nothing clears a porch of napping cats like the appearance of a human with the flea spray or ear mite drops in hand.

If you ever need to give a pill to a cat- see the handy directions at the end of this article- these directions have traveled the world over, and I tried to find the original author, but had no luck. My best guess is that he/she has been quietly committed.

So, why DO we keep cats around, when we could accomplish mouse control via a visit to our pest control aisle at the Farm and Fleet?

Well…. in addition to catching mice, there is a theory that cats keep the population of snakes in the house/barn in check. Not that they hunt snakes. They don't. But since cats are by nature into, under, on top of, and behind EVERYTHING, it makes for precious few peaceful hidey-holes for snakes to, well, hole up in. And snakes love peace, so are less apt to hang around where there is cat activity.

I have a friend who runs a boarding kennel who swears that fleas prefer cats over dogs, and when she gets fleas on the dogs in the kennel, she tosses her unflappable house cat in there for a day. She claims that the dogs are then flea-free and the only critter she has to treat is the cat. Dubious, but makes for some interesting mental images.

Oh, there are the Normal Rockwellian reasons for keeping cats- think of every image of a successful, peaceful happy farm- a cat dozing in the hay loft, a cat gazing contentedly into the fireplace, cats following the milkmaid to the barn, cats draped over front porch furniture like furry doilies.

I suspect that the real reason many of us keep farm cats is exactly because we aren't KEEPING them. Everyone else on the farm is being held there by physical barriers through the use of fencing or coops (goats, dogs, chickens, horses) or by mental barriers through the use of legal contracts or age deficiencies (spouses and children).

In spite of their aloof attitude, so different from dogs (dogs look at you like you hung the moon, cats look at you like you just flashed them the moon) cats stay for one reason.

Just because they feel like it.

Instructions for giving your cat a pill

1) Pick cat up and cradle it in the crook of your left arm as if holding a baby. Position right forefinger and thumb on either side of cat's mouth and gently apply pressure to cheeks while holding pill in right hand. As cat opens mouth pop pill into mouth. Allow cat to close mouth and swallow.

2) Retrieve pill from floor and cat from behind sofa. Cradle cat in left arm and repeat process.

3) Retrieve cat from bedroom, and throw soggy pill away.

4) Take new pill from foil wrap, cradle cat in left arm holding rear paws tightly with left hand. Force jaws open and push pill to back of mouth with right forefinger. Hold mouth shut for a count of ten.

5) Retrieve pill from goldfish bowl and cat from top of wardrobe. Call friend.

6) Kneel on floor with cat wedged firmly between knees, hold front and rear paws. Ignore low growls emitted by cat. Get friend to hold head firmly with one hand while forcing wooden ruler into

mouth. Drop pill down, remove ruler and rub cat's throat vigorously.

7) Retrieve cat from curtain rail, get another pill from foil wrap. Make note to buy new ruler and repair curtains. Carefully sweep shattered Doulton figures from hearth and set to one side for gluing later.

8) Wrap cat in large towel and get friend to lie on cat with head just visible from below armpit. Put pill in end of drinking straw, force cat's mouth open with pencil and blow down drinking straw.

9) Check label to make sure pill is not harmful to humans, drink glass of water to take taste away. Apply band-aid to friend's forearm and remove blood from carpet with cold water and soap.

10) Retrieve cat from neighbor's shed. Get another pill. Place cat in cupboard and close door onto neck to leave head showing. Force mouth open with dessertspoon. Flick pill down throat with elastic band.

11) Fetch screwdriver from garage and put cupboard door back on hinges. Apply cold compress to cheek and check records for date of last tetanus shot. Throw Tee shirt away and fetch new one from bedroom.

12) Ring fire brigade to retrieve cat from tree across the road. Apologize to neighbor who crashed into fence while swerving to avoid cat. Take last pill from foil-wrap.

13) Tie cat's front paws to rear paws with garden twine and bind tightly to leg of dining table, find heavy duty pruning gloves from shed, hold cat's mouth open with small spanner. Push pill into mouth followed by large piece of fillet of steak. Hold head vertically and pour pint of water down throat to wash pill down.

14) Get friend to drive you to the emergency room, sit quietly while doctor stitches fingers and forearm and removes pill

remnants from right eye. Call furniture shop on way home to order new table.

15) Arrange for SPCA* to collect cat. Ring local pet shop to see if they have any hamsters.

Compare the above with

Instructions for giving your Dog a pill-

1) Stuff it into a piece of cheese.

Keeping the Homestead Dream Alive- What to Do When the Bluebird of Happiness Poops on Your Head

There are a few, a lucky few, folks who were born on the family farm, grew up on the family farm, learned how to run the family farm, and have no doubt about where they will live and what they will do- they will continue the family farm.

For the rest of us, the road to our Homestead is usually not so direct. Fraught with detours, dead ends and missing road signs, sometimes it takes years to get ‘there’, and once there, sometimes, like the dream where you think you are at the bottom, but you just keep falling, our final destination remains elusive.

Perhaps your earliest memories include fantasies of ponies, hen houses and amber waves of grain, or maybe in an otherwise normal adulthood one day pushing pencils in your cubicle you were seized with the overwhelming urge to leap out the window and go plant something. Outside. In the dirt. And the sunshine. And never be ‘cubed’ again.

No matter- the result is the same- the need and desire to claim a bit of earth, raise a barn, fill it with food-on-the-hoof nourished by grass-in-the-pasture, and earn your keep by the sweat of your brow, darn it.

Tis a worthy goal, and like all worthy goals, there must be a worthy plan- a neat and well thought out plan that takes you from point A, to point B and all the way to point Q, which is right about where your farm sits, a perfect jewel set into the warm bosom of a blissful countryside.

Point A is deceptively easy. It consists of “I wanna be a homesteader.”

Point B is substantially more involved, and quite a bit more lengthy, but generally fun and relatively inexpensive and painless. This is where all the preliminary learning is done. Your collection of magazines, books, bookmarked websites and business cards will amaze even yourself in an alarmingly short time. New words and phrases will roll off your tongue leaving your ears wondering, "who said that?" Sustainability, Grass-fed Beef, and Nitrogen Fixing Cover Crops- these and other until-now odd combinations of words will dance through your head at night like visions of sugarplums.

The whole concept seems so right. Caring for the earth while caring for your family, dying a noble peaceful death and being cared for in turn by the earth, like our ancestors did for generation upon generation. Shunning the mainstream belief of the nine to five followed by the 401k, we voraciously devour every tale telling how others have accomplished this modern day return to a basic and good life.

And one shining truth shimmers through each family story according to the published word- simply follow your plan (or THEIR plan, if they are selling a book), and the end result will be your homestead. Happy smiling family waving from a tractor on the last page, The End.

For most of us, this couldn't be a crueler fallacy.

Because somewhere after Point B, life gets in the way. People lose jobs, they lose spouses, they gain a child or responsibility of a parent or grandparent, there's a chronic illness or debilitating injury tossed into the mix and the lovely plan is in shatters, tatters and shreds.

This is where we separate the wheat from the chaff, the rice from the hulls, the peanuts from the butter. At this juncture, some people will decide that the homesteading dream is just that- a pretty dream, like the one where Antonio Banderas rides up on a black stallion, swoops you off your feet, hands you a perfectly frozen Dove bar (not too hard, but not dripping and mooshy either) and gallops off to sunny Mexico with you to the perfect beach with sand that will never get into your ice cream…

Ahem. Sorry…

The "homesteading as a pretty dream" group will buck up, re-group and move on.

The others. Ah, the others. Every fragment of a thought inference that they will never have their piece of earth will result in the sound of a tiny piece of their heart breaking.

This story is for you, my friends.

There is ALWAYS something you can do that will move you in the right direction, and just because you APPEAR to be moving backwards, does not mean that you must STAY moving backwards.

Although the causes of Homestead Dream Endangerment are many, the results are basically the same few depression inducing scenarios-

Dream Endangerment Scenario One- Stuck in the City- No Money to Get Out.

This one is the hardest because it's like you are smacked down even before you get started. In actuality, this is where you can hone skills before you need them. Go to the farmers' market, buy a bunch of veggies and fruits and teach yourself to freeze, dehydrate and can. Learn to bake bread. Find and take classes on sewing, knitting, woodworking, basic carpentry, electrical and plumbing, heck even car repair (tractors have engines- who knew?).

If you only have a yard, you can have a garden- plant veggies in between your flowers, veggies are plants too. If you have only a balcony, you can have a few pots with tomato and pepper plants in them, and smaller pots with herbs around them (if you have oregano, basil and cilantro, you have spaghetti sauce and salsa. What more could you want?).

Volunteering and visiting working farms is a good way to figure out for sure and for certain what you like and what you hate about different aspects of farming, and is more likely to be done BEFORE you leap in with both rubber boots on. Finding out that your elaborate and brilliant plan to raise heritage Widget Sheep is going to be more difficult than you imagined because you have a previously unknown allergy to lanolin, is something better learned early on.

Of course all this is done in your 'spare time', while trimming your budget and working overtime to truly be able to escape the city once you find your property. Which brings us to

Dream Endangerment Scenario Two- Land Land Everywhere, But Not a Farm in Sight

Tiny sweat covered down payment in hand, it's time to find your land and stake your claim to it. If you know where you want to settle, it's hard enough- even in the flattest part of the world, the difference between parcels of land is astounding. If you are considering moving somewhere you've never been before, it's mind-boggling.

The first 100 or so parcels that you look at will be fun and educational. After that it just gets tediously bizarre, like that old Dunkin Donuts commercial where the baker sleepwalks to work every morning at 3am chanting "time to make the donuts. Time to make the donuts", you will drive down little back roads, map in hand droning "gotta find the land. Gotta find the land".

This is the danger zone- and you must remember three key words- Do Not Settle. No matter what, wait till you step onto the piece of land that whispers to your soul and you will make a happy home and farm there, regardless of any apparent limitations it may have. (Of course this is taking for granted that you will automatically pass on any land that includes a toxic waste dump, has no source of water, or swarms with werewolves every full moon). Once you've found your land, you must make it yours which usually involves jumping through hoops for men in suits and

Dream Endangerment Scenario Three- Banks Only Lend Money to Those Who Don't Need It

A lot of us are credit challenged, and most of us are not, despite what our Credit Score screams, deadbeats. Job loss, sickness, divorce- any number of things can launch the most conscientious person straight out of the mainstream financial institutions for a mortgage. Several factors make this worse- if you are relocating across country there will be no local references for employment or residence. This makes bankers nervous. And if the land in question is no barn- no house nekkid, they will really start twitching.

Historically, they have a point. If something in your life gets tough and you need to pick and choose what and who gets paid, you will keep your house that you live in current. You will keep your vehicle that you need to get to work current. Banks assume that if the going gets tough, you will start skipping your land note, and they are usually right. Even though bankers enjoy being right, they dislike foreclosing on properties- a lot of paperwork and court orders and sheriffs involved there and they'd just as soon avoid it, so they don't make the loans to begin with.

The options are to either cough up enough of a down payment to make it worth their while (and simultaneously gagging on a killer interest rate), or find someone to owner-carry, at least till you can get some stability established. Once the bank has a record of a year or so of timely made payments and knows you are not going to leave them holding a partially improved farm, they will generally consider re-writing your note at a more attractive rate. If you do go 'owner carry', make sure ANY owner-carry note is drawn up by a lawyer to avoid 'misunderstandings' down the line.

When you have closed on the land and have moved out yonder, a lot of folks are faced with

Dream Endangerment Scenario Four- Well, Here We Are, But Now We Can't Afford to Do a Dang Thing

Patience.
Start small.
Caution.
Resist the temptations of mental, physical or financial over-extension
Or sure as shootin' you will find yourself smack dab in the middle of

Dream Endangerment Scenario Five- How Did We Manage To Lose The Farm?

Of course there are many routes to this unfortunate spot, and most of them do not have anything to do with your intelligence, money management or farming savvy. There are many times the excrement contacts the oscillator and you either get angry, or you get over it. If you know in your heart that you have done the best you know how, and in the cases where there WERE misjudgments, you learned from them and are determined not to repeat them, this is not a terminal scenario.

Let's talk about me for a minute (and I promise Antonio Banderas is not part of this, but I make no such vow about the Dove bars).

I was born and raised up in a mid sized town in Wisconsin.
Got married.
Learned everything I could about country life while my first child was a toddler.
Moved out to 3 acres when I was pregnant with my second child.
Got a big garden going, dairy goats and horses.
Divorced 7 years later and lost the farm.
Married again.
Packed the U-Haul and drove to Texas.
Did several years time in the Worst Trailer Park in Texas.
Got divorced again.
Moved into a 'fixer upper' on 3 acres.
Got a garden going, dairy goats, horses and poultry.

Married again and had another child.
Decided 3 acres is too small, so looked and looked and finally found 12 acres.
Jumped through roughly 10,000 hoops before securing financing.
Started planning new family farm that centers around building our own home, ourselves.
Family encounters serious health issues.
Farm plan re-worked to include local contractor as a principal character to achieve building goals.
Everyone enjoys a Dove bar.

My story is not that unusual, and certainly does not include insurmountable problems. I can think of at least half a dozen of my friends who have done so much more with seemingly so much less. At some point all of us have wrestled with

Dream Endangerment Scenario Six- I'm Too Danged Old to Do This

If this thought enters your mind the answer is YES- you ARE too old to do this the same way you planned it in your teens, twenties and thirties. But if you re-work the labor parts, and smallen the day-to-day workload, you'll find that homesteading is not out of reach, you just have to shift your definition of a successful farm.

The common thread among us is the bullheadedness to not give up when most sane folks would. Whether that makes us sensible is up for debate. But that really matters not.

Because no matter where we are physically or financially, our hearts and our minds are on the farm, and nothing can take that away from us.

Whether we are growing beans behind the petunias, or canning veggies in a high rise, you can take the homesteader out of the country,

But you can never take the country out of the homesteader.

Sheri Dixon lives in the pineywoods of East Texas with her family of assorted two and four legged critters.

Most of her time is spent cleverly discovering all the things NOT to do in the running of a successful small family farm.

Easterchicks Gone Bad is her second book.

Please visit her at www.sheri-dixon.com

www.ingramcontent.com/pod-product-compliance
Lightning Source LLC
LaVergne TN
LVHW051629080426
835511LV00016B/2246

* 9 7 8 0 6 1 5 6 7 7 5 6 9 *